"The only book in the world that teaches how to apply the miraculous Ho'oponopono technique in the simplest way possible for anything from healing to manifestation to practical life solutions"

An
Intelligent
Adult

ANKIT YADAV

BLUEROSE PUBLISHERS
India | U.K.

Copyright © Ankit Yadav 2024

All rights reserved by author. No part of this publication may be reproduced, stored in a retrieval system or transmitted in any form or by any means, electronic, mechanical, photocopying, recording or otherwise, without the prior permission of the author. Although every precaution has been taken to verify the accuracy of the information contained herein, the publisher assumes no responsibility for any errors or omissions. No liability is assumed for damages that may result from the use of information contained within.

BlueRose Publishers takes no responsibility for any damages, losses, or liabilities that may arise from the use or misuse of the information, products, or services provided in this publication.

For permissions requests or inquiries regarding this publication, please contact:

BLUEROSE PUBLISHERS
www.BlueRoseONE.com
info@bluerosepublishers.com
+91 8882 898 898
+4407342408967

ISBN: 978-93-6261-150-5

Cover design: Shivam
Typesetting: Namrata Saini

First Edition: August 2024

With the Grace of Guru
(गुरू कृपा)

I dedicate my work to my grandfather Shree Ratiram Yadav (Retd. Headmaster), Writer of anonymous spiritual literary work "Aatmabodh" and yet to be published "Kabir Geeta" among others. His teachings and lifelong habits of reading, learning and writing inspired me to present this masterpiece before you.

To my Parents for their blessing in my every endeavour.

To my younger sister Ritika for her playful yet kind gestures of tease and support.

To my family, friends, colleagues and loved ones.

I present my gratitude to the almighty God.

Thank You.

Disclaimer

The content in this book is intended for informational purposes only and has been derived from various sources. It also contains personal views of the author that may or may not match the views of the reader. Readers acknowledge that neither the publisher nor the author are engaging in the rendering of legal, financial, medical, or professional advice or services to the individual reader. The ideas, procedures, and suggestions contained in this book are not intended as a substitute for consulting with your physician. All matters regarding your health require medical supervision. By reading this book, the reader agrees that under no circumstances is the author responsible for any losses, direct or indirect, which are incurred as a result of the use of information contained within this book, including, but not limited to, — errors, omissions, or inaccuracies.

Contents

Chapter-1: Catch on to Yourself and Others Better 1

"Ketsueki-gata"-The Blood Group Personality 4
Numerology 9
Astrology 17
Ayurveda 25
Homeopathy 30
Samudrik Shastra 34

Chapter-2: The Energy Thing 37

The Hermetic Philosophy:- 39
The 12 Laws of The Universe :- 44
The Law of Attraction (LOA) 58
Understanding the Key Components of the LOA :- 68
Common hindrances while practicing Law of Attraction:- 75
Manifestation with Water technique 80

Chapter-3: Ho'oponopono -A Magical Mantra 82

How to Practice "Ho'oponopono" ? 84
Ho'oponopono and Law of Attraction 85
Hoponoopono for happy relationships 88
Ho'oponopono for Desired Health 89
Ho'oponopono For Career and money 91
Ho'oponopono for Meetings and interviews 93
Ho'oponopono For Any Desire 94
Ho'oponopono to heal someone 96

Ho'oponopono For Non living things 98
Ho'oponopono For contentment 99

Chapter-4: Discipline 101

Hurdles in the way to discipline:- 103
Strategies to overcome procrastination 105
How distractions can derail discipline 106
Strategies for Overcoming Hurdles 107

Chapter-5: The Pomodoro Technique 110

How does Pomodoro technique works? 112

Chapter-6: Living in the present moment 113

Chapter-7: Ever Living in a state of Joy 116

Chapter-8: Habits of an intelligent adult 124

Chapter-9: Quotes and poems by author 133

References and Citations 147

CHAPTER-1

Catch on to Yourself and Others Better

In order to master the world, firstly one should master oneself. And how one will be able to master the self? To win or master something, the very first step that should be taken is to know the thing or skill that you want to excel and master. One of the most appropriate and practical ways to know the self is continuous observation of likes, interests, dislikes, urges, actions and certain reactions given to them.

The biggest hurdle I see nowadays in knowing ourselves is very easy access to stimulations. Stimulations doesn't allow us to think about ourselves and don't let us to feel that positive sense of urgency which makes you motivated to achieve something meaningful in life. Technology plays the role of easy to accessible and cheap source of stimulation for youth nowadays. The energy which should be channelize into productive and creative work is getting wasted as being a couch potato doing nothing and self gratification has worked as fuel into fire by making everything as new normal for us. The technology which was created to make our lives easy, comfortable and more productive is enslaving us and making us compelled day by day. Since the advancement of technology, man has got degraded it's natural strength and capabilities. The purpose is not to criticise modern advancements but to utilise them smartly as a tool of productivity and strength.

Continuous and conscious observation of the self, helps to know ourselves better which in turn helps to know about our strengths, weaknesses and also the productive fields on which we should work on in our life. Self-knowing and self-mastery also helps to find and decide your purpose in life and once someone knows oneself better that person is not affected by the opinions of others and hence saves his/her energy by overcoming the negative feelings of stress, anxiety and social pressures, that person can live life on his terms, can choose what's good for her and can lead her life in a well-chosen and self-determined directions. And by knowing the self you also develop a very good quality that is to understand other persons and their instincts better and then it becomes a tough task to make a fool out of you as well as taking advantage of you will not be an easy game for anyone.

As we discussed that continuous and conscious observation is a very good practical and appropriate psychological method to know someone and something easily. Psychology, the scientific study of the mind and the way that people behave has so much to say about yourself.

Although there are many theories and works of many different psychologists regarding different personality types. For example Myers-Briggs Type Indicator (MBTI), Enneagram, etc.

But most modern-day psychologists agree that there are five major personality types:-

1. Conscientiousness.

People having this trait have good level of organization, responsibility, and reliability. These People are efficient and well-organized, dependable, and self-sufficient. They plan things in advance and aim for high achievement. People who lack this personality type may view those with this personality trait as stubborn and obsessive.

Fun fact: Studies show being in company with a person high in conscientiousness increases your chances of success at workplace. A conscientious spouse or friend can boost your productivity and help you achieve the most in life.

2. Extroversion.

This trait shows an individual's level of sociability, assertiveness, and outgoingness. These People gain energy from social activity. They're talkative and outgoing and they're well going in the spotlight. Other People may view them as domineering and attention-seekers.

Fun fact: Aware of the strong handshake next time. Men of this personality have strong handgrips, they are less neurotic However it is not true in the case of women.

3. Agreeableness.

This type of individuals are good at cooperativeness, empathy, and consideration for others. These people are trustworthy, kind, and affectionate toward others. They're known for their pro-social behavior (behaviour through which people benefit others) and they're often committed to volunteer work and noble activities. Other people often see them as naive and overly passive.

Fun fact: financial investor with this personality types are least likely to lose money from risky trading. Whereas investor high in openness are generally overconfident and hence they take excessive risks.

4. Openness to Experience.

These people have a good degree of imagination, creativity, and openness to new ideas and experiences. They are known for their broad range of interests and vivid imaginations. These people are curious and creative and they usually prefer variety over rigid routines. They're known for their pursuits of self-actualization through intense, euphoric experiences. Others may view them as hard to predict and unfocused.

Fun fact: People with this personality type consistently predicts political orientation. They endorse liberalism and express their political beliefs more often.

5. Neuroticism.

These people often feel emotionally instable, anxious and moody. Neurotic people experience a high degree of emotional instability. They're more likely to be reactive and excitable and they report higher degrees of unpleasant emotions like anxiety and irritability. They may seem as unstable and insecure to other people.

Fun fact: These people seek acceptance mostly via uploading lot of pictures on social media platforms. They don't like to engage in controversies.

Along with it there are many more methods and sciences in different cultures and different regions of world which makes you conscious about yourself and others in your surroundings.

"Ketsueki-gata"-The Blood Group Personality

In many countries, including India, people usually take a close look at a potential partner's star sign to check their compatibility level. But the Japanese like to do things a little differently. They do not rely on the astrological information and signs alone, rather on the blood type for personality matching and information. Yes, your blood group can reveal your personality type!

"Ketsueki-gata" is a term that originated in Japan and refers to a personality typing system based on a person's blood type. The idea is that a person's blood type can determine their personality traits, strengths, and weaknesses. The term gained popularity since the 1930s, thanks to Japanese professor Tokeji Furukawa who published a paper claiming that each blood type reflected the personality of a person who possessed it.

You will be surprised to know that in Japan people are very fond of asking the blood type of other people because they truly believe in blood type personality theory. Japanese people use it as a tool to assess the potential of an employee and the compatibility of two people getting married.

1. **Type A:** Considered to be calm, patient, and reliable, but also perfectionists who can be overly sensitive and anxious.

People with A blood type are sensitive, cooperative, emotional, passionate and clever. They are very patient, loyal and love peace and thus do not like to get into a fight with anyone. But sometimes these people become overly sensitive. They do not like to break the rules set down by society and care about etiquette and social standards.

These people take their time to make decisions and are too organized in all spheres of life but cannot multitask. They like things neat and clean and at the right place, which is why many people with OCD (Obsessive Compulsive Disorder) fall into A blood type.

People with this blood type also get stressed easily and thus have a high level of cortisol (stress) hormone.

Common personality traits: Kind, shy, attentive, stubborn, polite, tensed, reliable, overly sensitive, perfectionist, responsible, timid, anxious, composed and reserved.

Positive personality traits: Loyal, perfectionists, organized and consistent.

Negative personality traits: Obsessive, overly sensitive, pessimistic, stubborn, easily stressed and fastidious.

These people make reliable and trustworthy friends. They do not like to show their emotions and feeling to anyone unless they are comfortable with them. Famous people with blood type A include Narendra Modi, George Bush, Jet Li, Britney Spears, and Richard Nixon.

2. **Type B:** Considered to be creative, flexible, and passionate, but also selfish, unpredictable, and impulsive.

People with the B blood type may be more likely to be creative individuals. Individuals who have B blood may make their decisions quickly, and they are not good at taking orders. When type B blood people focus on something, they put their all into it, and they are unlikely to let go, even if the goal seems unachievable or impractical. People with a B blood type can have a very strong drive or desire to be the best at anything that they have set their minds to do. Nevertheless, according to blood type personality theory, people with this blood type are poor at multitasking. They are likely to neglect other important tasks and put all their focus on whatever they have set their mind on at the moment.

B blood type people might face a lot of discrimination because of their potential negative personality traits, such as a tendency to be more selfish or uncooperative and stubborn at times. Society mainly focuses on the negative side of people with blood type B, even though people with this blood type (like any person) have many good qualities, too. As a result, they may tend to be loners, and may isolate themselves from others more so than other blood types.

Blood type personality theory states that they may tend to approach things at their own pace. Some of the most common traits of people with blood type B include the following:

Positive personality traits: Curious, strong, relaxed, creative, adventurous, passionate, cheerful, active and outgoing.

Negative personality traits: Wild, erratic, selfish, unforgiving, uncooperative, irresponsible and unpredictable.

Famous people with type B include Vince Young, Leonardo DiCaprio, and Jack Nicholson. Albert Einstein, considered to be the greatest physicist of the 20th century, is said to have had blood type B.

3. **Type AB:** Considered to be a mix of A and B types, often described as rational yet emotional, adaptable yet shy, and confident yet indecisive.

People with AB blood type are a mix of A and B personality types, just like their blood group. These people are complicated and can have dual personalities like they can be shy like A type as well as outgoing like B type. They try to keep their true personalities from strangers, thereby making most believe that they are a mixed personality. It is hard to decode these people until you know them thoroughly. Also, these people are the rarest blood type in the world.

They are charming and make friends easily. There will never be a dull moment in a group of friends even if only one of them is AB blood type. They are poor at handling stress.

AB people are very careful while dealing with others and are empathetic. These people also have exceptional analytical and logical skills.

Positive personality traits: Charming, controlled, cool, dream chaser, caring, rational, trustworthy, adaptable and creative.

Negative personality traits: Complicated, vulnerable, irresponsible, self-centered, forgetful, unforgiving and critical.

Famous people with AB blood types include Barack Obama, Marilyn Monroe, Jackie Chan, and John F. Kennedy.

4. **Type O:** Considered to be confident, sociable, and outgoing, but also stubborn and insensitive.

People with blood type O are considered to be outgoing, go-getters, and daring. Blood type personality theory states that they usually set high standards for themselves, and they do all they can to achieve them. Blood type O have excellent leadership capabilities. Little things do not concern them, and this may make them appear selfish to people in blood group A who may be overly sensitive.

Some of the positive personality traits in people with blood type O include the following:

Positive personalities traits: Leadership, easy going, positive outlook, confident, calm, outgoing, cautious, loyal, peaceful, passionate, independent, reliable, carefree, trendsetter and devoted.

Negative personality traits: Jealous, ruthless, rude, non-punctual, insensitive, cold, unpredictable, self-centered and arrogant.

Individuals with blood type O are very enduring and strong, and that is why the Japanese call them warriors. They are honest people and despise people who tell a lie or hide the truth. People who are O are not overly cautious about small details, as they tend to focus more on the big picture. Famous people with blood type O include Queen Elizabeth II, Paul Newman, Elvis Presley, Ronald Regan, John Gotti, and Gerald Ford.

According to the theory:-

Blood Group	**Compatible Blood Group**
Type A	With Type A and AB
Type B	With Type B and AB
Type O	With Type AB and O
Type AB	With All Types (A, B, AB, O)

In Japan, blood type is often believed to be an indicator of personality traits, similar to how astrological signs are viewed in the West.

Meanwhile, in the U.S., blood type personality has been given less importance than the diseases associated with different blood group types.

Numerology

Numerology is a belief system that assigns significance to numbers, based on the idea that numbers have mystical properties and can reveal information about a person's character, personality, and future events. It is a form of divination, which involves seeking insight or guidance from supernatural sources.

Numerology involves reducing numbers to their single-digit form by adding the digits together. For example, the number 23 would be reduced to 2+3=5. Each number is then assigned specific meanings or characteristics, and the resulting number sequence can be interpreted to reveal insights into a person's personality or future events.

Numerology has a long history, with roots in various cultures and religions including ancient Babylon, Greece, and China. It is often associated with the teachings of Pythagoras, a Greek philosopher and mathematician who believed that numbers had mystical properties and could reveal hidden truths about the universe.

The numerology most frequently practiced today is based on the teachings of the ancient Greek philosopher, Pythagoras. Pythagoras was a brilliant mathematician, but he wasn't just interested in quantitative solutions. He believed that the physical world was the amalgamation of the energetic vibrations of numbers, and developed a system that corresponded letters with integers. This practice was a study of numerical interconnectivity — the belief that everything is aligned through non-physical forces best articulated through numbers.

Your Life Path Number

The easiest way to start working with numerology is by analyzing your unique date of birth. Numerology is all about getting to the root number. To do this, you simply reduce digits until you reach a single-digit number, excluding 11 and 22, which are considered Master Numbers. This single digit is your individual Life Path Number.

The Life Path Number is similar to your Sun Sign in astrology: It reveals your identity, including strengths, weaknesses, talents, and ambitions. Your Life Path Number also exposes the tone of your experiences, and why events occur past, present, and future. Simply put, it creates an organized, structured system that illuminates your lived experiences.

Let's say your birthday is March 3, 1999. To calculate your Life Path Number, you will reduce each component of this date to a single digit:

The month, 3, remains a single digit = 3.

The date, 3, also remains a single digit = 3.

The year, 1999, is reduced to 1 + 9 + 9+ 9. This equals 28. Then, 28 is reduced to 2 + 8= 10, which again reduced to 1 + 0= 1.

Then, we add the reduced month, date, and year numbers (3 + 3 + 1) and arrive at 7. Which is already a single digit number. If you were born on March 3, 1999, your Life Path Number is 7.

Isn't that easy to find?

Now Let's move to the concept of Master No's in Numerology.

Master Numbers in Numerology

The only time you don't have to reduce the final number is when you attain 11 or 22 as the final numbers. Because these two no's are considered as master numbers and they signify more intensified version of the root numbers of both the master numbers that is (1+1=2 and 2+2=4)

For example, Sir Paul McCartney, Probably England's most famous Gemini, was born on June 18, 1942. When this date is reduced (month = 6, day = 9, year = 7), the sum is 22. Now we won't reduce the final sum into a single digit which is

(2+2=4) because here the number 22 denotes a master number which reveals McCartney's strong "life mission."

Your Destiny Number in Numerology

You can also use numerology to derive the root number of names or words. Pythagoras guides us in this. According to his theories, certain letters have specific numerical values, which are as follows:

Letters	Number
A, J, S	1
B, K, T	2
C, L, U	3
D, M, V	4
E, N, W	5
F, O, X	6
G, P, Y	7
H, Q, Z	8
I, R	9

Using this technique, it's easy to find the root number associated with names, which numerologists refer to as your Destiny Number. To find your Destiny Number, calculate the root number of your full name (first, middle, last) by reducing each name to a single digit, and adding up the total.

For example, my full name (Ankit Yadav) reveals my Destiny Number: ANKIT (1 + 5 + 2 + 9 + 2 = 19, which becomes 1 + 9 = 10 which further becomes 1 + 0 = 1) YADAV (7 + 1 + 4 + 1 + 4 = 17, which becomes 1 + 7 = 8), resulting in a Destiny Number of 9 (because 1 + 8 = 9).

Whereas your Life Path reveals your greater purpose, your Destiny Number offers insight as to how you will express your greater goals. Now find yours and check how much do they resonate?

What Numerology Says About Your Number?

So, now that you've calculated your Life Path Number and Destiny Number, it's time to find out what these digits really mean. Let's take a closer look!

Number 1 (10/1, 19/1)

The number 1 is linked to forward motion in Numerology. 1 symbolizes a pioneering spirit, independent nature, and innate leadership capabilities. On some days 1 can be a bit bossy or boastful. They hide their insecurities behind over-developed self-importance. Although it is the first number, 1s must take care that they can very quickly become the loneliest.. Even the most autonomous 1s need the support of their friends, family, and lovers.

Number 2 (11/2, 20/2)

The number 2 is linked to sensitivity, balance, and harmony. Within numerology, the 2 vibration assumes the role of the mediator, creating harmony by bringing together dissonant forces through compassion, empathy, and kindness. 2 is linked to psychic abilities and intuition, and if this number appears as a Life Path or Destiny Number, the individual will be very clever to judge the subtle energy shifts and emotional nuances. Because 2 is so sensitive, it is very conflict-averse, and can end up feeling under-appreciated or unacknowledged. 2 must avoid seeking external validation and, instead, realize that perfect equilibrium needed already exists within.

Number 3 (12/3, 21/3)

Communication is paramount for 3. Symbolically, 3 represents the output of two joined forces: It is the essence of creation. 3

is highly gifted at expression, seamlessly sharing innovative and pioneering concepts through art, writing, and oration. Your work inspires, motivates, and uplifts others, and 3 finds great joy making others smile. However, 3 is also known to be quite moody, and if 3 feels misunderstood, may withdraw entirely. The escapist tendencies of 3 are easily mitigated by practicing peaceful mindfulness: With such an active imagination, it's important for 3 to find moments of quiet to reset, restore, and recharge.

Number 4 (13/4, 22/4, 31/4)

In numerology, 4 has an earthy-energy and is centered around fortifying its roots. 4 adamantly believes in the physical world and knows that investing in a solid infrastructure is necessary for building a lasting legacy. Practical, hardworking, and responsible, the vibration of the number 4 is focused on creating logical systems that can support scalable growth. There is a solidity to 4, however, that can quickly devolve into rigidity; 4 must remember that rules are meant to enhance, not inhibit. It's easy for 4 to become stubborn, so 4 benefits from learning to loosen up and think outside the box. 4 will feel liberated and inspired by finding the bravery to take a few bold risks.

Number 5 (14/5, 23/5, 32/5)

Free-thinking, adventurous, and progressive, 5 is defined by freedom. 5 needs to experience the world by engaging its five senses: For 5, life lessons are acquired through spontaneous acts of bravery. Akin to Sagittarius Energy within astrology, 5 is known for its playful, impulsive, and vivacious spirit. But on the other side of its signature joie de vivre (Cheerfulness), 5 can become restless and impatient. Since 5 is always seeking discovery, it has a difficult time accepting life's day-to-day responsibilities — including professional and interpersonal commitments. 5 must remember that when it narrows its gaze, it will discover that the most rewarding exploration exists in its own backyard.

Number 6 (15/6, 24/6, 33/6)

6 is recognized for its nurturing, supportive, and empathic nature. A true healer, 6 has the ability to solve problems in both the emotional and physical realms, helping others through its straightforward, yet gentle, approach. 6 has a strong sense of responsibility and cares deeply for its friends, family, and lovers. This number also can easily communicate with children and animals, displaying a soft tenderness and caretaker spirit. But not everything needs to be parented, and sometimes 6's protective energy can become domineering and controlling. To avoid carrying the world on its shoulders, 6 must learn to build trust and understanding for others: Simply put, everyone must follow their own unique path.

Number 7 (16/7, 25/7, 34/7)

The detectives of numerology, 7 is known for its investigative abilities and analytical skills. Astrologically, the number 7 can be thought of as a blend of Virgo and Scorpio energy: 7 is extremely detail-oriented, but is driven by inner-wisdom as opposed to tangible realities. 7 has a keen eye, and its astute observations fuel a quick-witted, inventive spirit. Because it can quickly find the flaws in almost any system, 7 is a bit of a perfectionist. 7 will often assume fault, so it's important for this number to counterbalance its inherent skepticism with an open mind. Not everything will be foolproof — but that's what makes life fun.

Number 8 (17/8, 26/8, 35/8)

8 is all about abundance. Within numerology, this number is linked to material wealth and financial success. Ambitious and

goal-oriented, 8 can effortlessly assume leadership positions through its natural magnetism. 8 applies big-picture thinking to broaden its scope, racing up the top of any ladder to reach extraordinary heights. But with great power comes great responsibility: 8 breeds workaholics, and on a bad day, can become excessively controlling and possessive. However, its negative qualities can be lessened by Giving Back to The Community. By using this success to help others, 8 realizes that there is nothing more valuable than contributing to the greater good.

Number 9 (18/9, 27/9, 36/9)

As the final single digit within numerology, 9 connotes an old soul. 9 is no stranger life's ups-and-downs of life — been there, done that. Accordingly, 9 can effortlessly synthesize large quantities of stimuli, psychically connecting the dots to form a cohesive whole. The mission for 9 is to reach its highest state of consciousness, and to help others also achieve this spiritual awareness. 9 isn't afraid to transform, and its malleable spirit inspires others to explore their own ranges of motion. Since 9, in many ways, has transcended the physical plane, it must constantly remember to anchor itself. 9 must learn to balance the abstract with the tangible, ultimately finding its place at the intersection of fantasy and reality.

Master Number 11 (11/2)

Master Number 11 revs up the energy of Number 2; its purpose is to heal the self and others through its elevated psychic abilities. Often, Master Number 11's intuitive gifts are a result of extreme life circumstances: Master Number 11 has no choice but to cultivate extrasensory talents. In numerology, Master Number 11 is connected to spiritual enlightenment, awareness, and philosophical balance.

Master Number 22 (22/4)

Master Number 22, often referred to as the Master Builder, expands on the vibrations of Number 4. Master Number 22 is inspired to create platforms in the physical realm that transcend immediate realities — by fusing the tangible and intangible, Master Number 22 cultivates a dynamic long-term legacy. Master Number 22's skills are usually a byproduct of early childhood instability that fuels innovative thought. Industrious, creative, and dependable, Master Number 22 is always on a mission to transform.

Although Science doesn't recognise numerology, many people find it interesting and use it as a tool for personal insight or guidance. It is often used in astrology, tarot, and other forms of divination to enhance their insights and predictions.

Astrology

As we see in India and there too specially in Hinduism, Astrology is a very popular ancient vedic science that suggests that the positions and movements of celestial bodies, such as planets and stars, can have an impact on human affairs and personalities. According to astrologers, the unique placement of these celestial bodies at the time of your birth can provide insights into your character, strengths, weaknesses, and potential life path.

Astrology typically uses your birth date, time, and location to create a personalized birth chart, which is a map of the positions of the planets and stars at the exact moment of your birth. This chart is then interpreted by an astrologer to provide insights into various aspects of your life, including your personality traits, your career path, your relationships, and your overall life purpose.

For example, your sun sign, which is determined by the position of the sun in the zodiac at the time of your birth, is often used to describe your basic personality traits. Your moon sign, which is based on the position of the moon in the zodiac, can provide insights into your emotional nature and inner self. Your rising sign can provide insights into your outer personality and how others perceive you.

What is Kundali in Astrology?

In astrology, Kundali (also known as a birth chart or natal chart) is a map of the positions of the planets and astrological houses at the time of an individual's birth. It is believed to be a crucial tool in Vedic astrology, a traditional system of astrology originating from ancient India.

The Kundali chart is divided into 12 houses, each representing different aspects of an individual's life such as their personality traits, career, health, relationships, and more. The planets' positions in the chart are believed to influence a person's life, and astrologers use this information to interpret and predict various events and tendencies in an individual's life.

Kundali is considered to be a powerful tool for self-discovery and understanding one's own strengths and weaknesses. Many people consult astrologers to have their Kundali prepared and interpreted, and use this information to make important decisions in their personal and professional lives. All you need is some very basic and general information about you and your birth and some good astrologer to make one kundali for you and you will be amazed by the information provided to you.

Planets in Astrology and in your Kundli

In astrology, planets are essential to the functioning of human life. Astronomy describes nine planets, while Vedic Astrology mentions seven primary planets. Astrology Planets have unique significance that impacts human existence. The Sun is the centre of our solar system, which is a gravitationally bound system made up of planets, asteroids, and other objects that orbit it. In addition to planets and other objects, the Solar System also includes the Asteroid Belt, which is situated between the planets Mars and Jupiter. Both positive and negative effects can be felt by "The Planet Earth" from all of these planets and objects.

The science known as Vedic Astrology is based on descriptions of the planets and their motions found in Vedas and other ancient writings from long ago. Our sages have already spoken about the planets and how they affect the world around us. Only seven major planets are thought to have an impact on the Earthly existence according to astrology. The following is a list of the seven major planets, arranged by distance from the sun in ascending order.

The Sun, also known as "The King Planet," is surrounded by the primary planets Mercury, Venus, Earth, Mars, Jupiter, and Saturn. In addition, a new object known as the "Moon" is added to Vedic Astrology as a planet. Although we all know that the Moon is a satellite of the planet Earth, its proximity to our planet has astrological effects on life on Earth as well. It is the primary object in the universe that has an impact on an individual's "Mind".

Nodes of Moon

Rahu and Ketu are the names of the two nodes that are defined in Vedic Astrology. "North node of the planet Moon" is Rahu, and "South node of the planet Moon" is Ketu. These are essentially regarded as the "Demon's" Head and Tail.

What are the planets in Astrology and how they affect the life on Earth?

The names of the two Moon nodes and the seven major planets have already been covered. We use the "Geocentric System" in Astrology, which holds that Earth is the centre of the universe and that the other major planets orbit it. The five planets represent these five vibrations – Jupiter for Space, Saturn for Air, Mars for Fire, Mercury for Earth, and Venus for Water. Let's now understand how these planets affect our lives astrologically:

- **Sun:** Known as the "King" of the Celestial Cabinet, the planet "Sun" Among all the planets, it is the hottest. It denotes the authority or status of the government in the community. It stands for our "Father" and "Soul". It gives all the planets their energy. Because of its brightness, the entire world is illuminated. It ascends in "Aries" and governs over "Leo" sign.

    It is said that the Sun is the soul of the planets. It is very strong, respectable, authoritative, and has many other great attributes. Sun will demonstrate how an individual reflects himself onto the world.

    Astrologically speaking, a strong Sun denotes authority and vitality, but a weak Sun can indicate egotism and a lack of confidence. When it comes to your career and profession, you might require a powerful Sun, but not when it comes to your personal connections.

    According to astrology, the sun is associated with the fire element, the dark red colour, the human race, the

Kshatriya caste, the vice planet, the Sattva guna, and the Pitta nature.

According to astrology, the sun governs the head, bones, eyes, heart, and brain. It stands for wheat, little trees, fruit-bearing trees, copper, and the father.

- **Moon:** It also goes by the title "Queen" of the Celestial Cabinet. In astrology, the moon is a symbol for the mind; it is thought to have a maternal influence on people, bestowing feelings of love, happiness, and positivity. Since the Moon represents the self in a kundli, its strength will benefit you at every stage of life. However, mental health issues like stress, depression, disinterest, etc. can be brought on by a weak Moon.

  Moon governs to the "Cancer" sign and gets exalted in "Taurus'.

  The nature of the moon in astrology: the moon is associated with the Vaisya caste, which is the business class. It symbolizes ladies, Vaat-Kapha nature, Sattva Guna, and favours white colour. That means if the Moon is weak in your Kundli, you have to wear white more often.

  According to astrology, the moon governs the mind, mother, art, eyesight, saliva, lungs, silver, rice, and the chest.

- **Mercury:** This planet is a reflection of "Prince" quality. Mercury is a planet that represents a person's capacity for reasoning or calculation. It covers mathematics and imparts "astrology" information as well.

  According to astrology, Mercury represents a person's humour, communication, intelligence, reasoning, and awareness. You must have understood that strong mercury favours education. It is given greater significance in the early stages of education.

The nature of Mercury in astrology: Mercury is the planet of the business class (Vaishya). It is a planet that belongs to the element earth and is neutral. The three natures of Vaat, Pitta, and Kapha are all present on Mercury. Green is the colour that Mercury loves. It rules over "Gemini" and "Virgo" signs in Astrology and gets exalted in "Virgo" sign.

Mercury is the planet of the maternal relatives, younger siblings and skin and sex-related illnesses. likewise it stands for trade, mathematics, speech, tongue, voice, dumbness, and laziness.

- **Venus:** Venus serves as a "Princess" in the Celestial Cabinet and is the planet that everyone seeks for. Venus is the sign of beauty, love, romance, and all relationships in one's life. In a man's birth chart, it also stands for the wife, girlfriend, or any other girl. It is also the marriage-related Karaka planet. It stands for a person's financial standing or status. It also has an effect on the relationship that one shares with their spouse and even business associates. Thus, a strong Venus in kundli favours professional life while a weak Venus is responsible for plagued love life and relationships. It is exalted in the Zodiac sign of Pisces and lords over the signs of Libra and Taurus.

Venus's nature in astrology: Venus belongs to the Brahmin caste and is beautiful, female. It represents water element, charm, Rajoguni and Kapha nature.

The colour that favours Venus is white and favours one's beauty, wife, love affair, sex, nuptial bliss(happiness in marriage), poetry, singing, eyes and women etc.

- **Mars:** The Celestial Cabinet's Commander in Chief or Soldier. Mars in astrology denotes courage, passion, bravery, strength and confidence. It demonstrates our aggression and fighting prowess. It gives us the bravery to face any circumstance. It is constantly in "Hurry" and prepared for battle. It demonstrates a person's "activeness" or "quick respond". For younger co-borns, police, army, surgeons, etc., it is a karaka planet. It becomes exalted in "Capricorn" and rules over "Aries" and "Scorpio".

- **Jupiter:** In the Celestial Cabinet, it serves as the "King's Minister." It stands for a person's wisdom. It also stands for the "Teachers" or "Gurus" who constantly enter our lives. In a woman's chart, it stands for the "Husband". It is a beneficent and pious planet. Jupiter helps the person excel in education and career. It stands for a person's family and children. It is ruled by "Sagittarius" and "Pisces" and becomes exalted in the Astrological sign of "Cancer."

- **Saturn:** The Celestial Cabinet's "Servant" It stands for the general people. This planet is renowned for its judgment. It assigns you grades based on the Karma you performed during current birth . It's a slow planet and takes time to provide you results. It demonstrates a person's "Patience". It's all about delaying things away. The planet Saturn represents the black colour. It has the air element to its name. It becomes weaker in "Aries" and elevated in "Libra". It governs the Zodiac Belt signs of Aquarius and Capricorn.

- **Rahu:** Despite not being a planet, it is essentially the Moon's northern node on the planet. "Chhaya Grah" or shadow planet is another name for it in Vedic Astrology. All it has is the Demon's Head. Rahu's curiosity over

"Worldly Fame" is constant. It constantly pursues materialistic goals. The name "Shanivrat Rahu" refers to the fact that it functions similarly to the planet "Saturn". Being a planet without a body, it is constantly in search of more and is never content with anything in any area of existence. Exaltation is thought to occur in "Taurus/Gemini" and debilitation in "Scorpio/Sagittarius". Rahu doesn't have a distinct sign; instead, it acts according to the sign and planet it's placed in.

- **Ketu:** It is also not a planet, it is referred to as the Moon's south node. It's the Demon's tail. Like Rahu, it is also a "Chhaya Grah". It has no interest in worldly fame and materialistic pursuits. It's simply the opposite of Rahu. This planet is highly spiritual and aims only for enlightenment. It all comes down to letting go of materialistic stuff. It's a planet with no head. In this incarnation, only Ketu is taken into consideration for Moksha. It reflects Sanchit Karma, past life karmas, and other things. Ketu is thought to act similarly to the planet "Mars". The sign of "Scorpio/Sagittarius" elevates it, while "Taurus/Gemini" debilitates it.

In the hour of need there is nothing wrong in consulting a good astrologer for really practical and helpful remedies. Overall, astrology can be a valuable tool for gaining self-awareness and understanding your strengths, weaknesses, and life path. However, it's important to remember that astrology is just one tool and should be used in conjunction with other methods of self-reflection and self-discovery.

Ayurveda

In Ayurveda, the traditional Indian system of medicine, human beings are believed to be composed of three fundamental doshas or energies, known as **Vata, Pitta, and Kapha**. Each individual has a unique combination of these doshas, known as their prakriti or constitution. The three prakritis and their associated personality traits are:

The three doshas and Prakritis associated with them

1. **Vata Prakriti**: In Ayurveda, Vata dosha is one of the three primary body-mind types, or doshas, that are believed to influence a person's physical, mental, and emotional characteristics. Vata is associated with the elements of air and ether and is responsible for movement, including nerve impulses, breathing, and circulation. Here are some characteristics of Vata dosha:

   - **Physical characteristics:** People with a Vata-predominant constitution are often thin, with a light build and dry, rough or cracked skin and their hairs and nails may be brittle. They may also have a tendency towards constipation, joint pain, and cold hands and feet and also feeling cold in general.

   - **Personality traits:** Individuals with dominant Vata dosha are typically creative, energetic, and enthusiastic. They are often quick-witted, spontaneous, flexible and adaptable and they enjoy exploring new ideas and experiences. They are often spontaneous, and may be described as having a lively or restless energy. However, they may also be prone to anxiety, nervousness, and indecisiveness.

- **Emotional tendencies:** Vata individuals are often sensitive, intuitive, empathetic and imaginative. They may be highly attuned to their emotions and the emotions of others. They enjoy new experiences. However, they may also be prone to feeling anxious, restless, or overwhelmed. They may have a tendency to worry excessively, and may struggle to quiet their minds and may also struggle with feeling grounded and connected. They may be prone to worry, fear, and feelings of insecurity.

- **Habits and preferences:** Vata individuals tend to have irregular eating and sleeping habits, and they may find it challenging to establish a routine. They tend to prefer light and easily digestible foods, and may enjoy foods that are warm, moist, and nourishing. They may also enjoy creative pursuits such as music, art, or writing.

- **Health tendencies:** Vata individuals may be prone to digestive issues such as gas, bloating, and constipation. They may also experience joint pain, stiffness, or cracking. They may have a tendency towards dry skin and hair, and may be prone to dehydration. Additionally, they may be more susceptible to anxiety disorders and nervous system disorders such as insomnia or ADHD.

- **Lifestyle recommendations:** To balance Vata dosha, Ayurveda recommends practices that promote warmth, stability, and routine. This may include regular meals, warm and grounding foods, gentle exercise, and regular sleep patterns. Vata individuals may also benefit from practices such as meditation, yoga, and self-massage to promote relaxation and reduce stress.

2. **Pitta Prakriti**: In Ayurveda, Pitta dosha is one of the three primary body-mind types, or doshas, that are believed to influence a person's physical, mental, and emotional characteristics. Pitta is associated with the elements of fire and water and is responsible for transformation and metabolism in the body. Here are some characteristics of Pitta dosha:

   - **Physical characteristics:** People with a Pitta-predominant constitution are often of medium build with a muscular and athletic physique, and they may have a tendency towards oily skin, acne, and premature graying or balding.

   - **Personality traits:** Individuals with dominant Pitta dosha are typically focused, driven, determined and ambitious. They are often organized, efficient, and analytical. They are often intelligent, analytical, and good problem-solvers. They may be passionate about their work or hobbies and have a strong desire to achieve their goals. However, they may also be prone to becoming overly competitive, aggressive or impatient. However, they may also be prone to anger, irritability, and perfectionism.

   - **Emotional tendencies:** Pitta individuals are often passionate, intense, strong-willed, confident and goal-oriented, but they may struggle with feeling overheated and burning out. They may be prone to frustration, impatience, and a critical attitude. They may have a tendency to become easily agitated, and may struggle to let go of their emotions.

   - **Habits and preferences:** Pitta individuals tend to have a strong appetite and a love for spicy, sour or salty foods. They may also enjoy engaging in competitive or challenging activities such as sports or debate. They tend to prefer cooler temperatures and may feel uncomfortable in hot or humid weather.

- **Health tendencies:** Pitta individuals may be prone to inflammatory conditions, such as acid reflux, ulcers, or skin rashes. They may also have a tendency towards high blood pressure or cholesterol. They may be more susceptible to stress-related disorders such as anxiety, insomnia, or migraines.

- **Lifestyle recommendations:** To balance Pitta dosha, Ayurveda recommends practices that promote coolness, calmness, and moderation. This may include cooling foods and drinks, regular exercise that is not too intense, and practices that promote relaxation and stress reduction such as meditation and spending time in nature. Pitta individuals may also benefit from expressing their creativity and spending time engaged in activities that they find enjoyable and fulfilling.

3. **Kapha Prakriti:** In Ayurveda, Kapha dosha is one of the three primary body-mind types, or doshas, that are believed to influence a person's physical, mental, and emotional characteristics. Kapha is associated with the elements of earth and water and is responsible for structure and lubrication in the body. Here are some characteristics of Kapha dosha:

    - **Physical characteristics:** People with a Kapha-predominant constitution are often of a larger build with a heavier and more robust physique, They often have a round, full face, large, lustrous eyes, and thick, luxurious hair. and they may have a tendency towards oily or smooth skin. Kapha individuals tend to have a slow digestive fire, which can lead to weight gain and sluggishness. They may also experience a tendency towards water retention and congestion.

- **Personality traits:** Individuals with dominant Kapha dosha are typically calm, steady, and compassionate. They are often nurturing, patient, and grounded. However, they may also be prone to lethargy, stubbornness, and resistance to change. Kapha people tend to have steady and enduring energy levels, but can be slow to get going in the morning. Kapha people enjoy routine and stability and may be resistant to change or new experiences. They also tend to enjoy food and may be prone to overeating. They may need motivation and encouragement to stay active and engaged in life.

- **Emotional tendencies:** Kapha individuals are often loving, caring, and empathetic, but they may struggle with feelings of attachment and possessiveness. They may be prone to depression, apathy, and lethargy.

- **Lifestyle recommendations:** To balance Kapha dosha, Ayurveda recommends practices that promote movement, stimulation, and lightness. This may include regular exercise that is vigorous, dry and light foods, and practices that promote mental and emotional stimulation such as socializing and pursuing creative projects. Kapha individuals may also benefit from practices such as fasting and detoxification to promote digestion and overall vitality.

Although each person has a dominant prakriti, they may also have varying degrees of the other two doshas. Additionally, factors such as diet, lifestyle, and environment can influence the balance of the doshas over time. The goal of Ayurveda is to achieve a balance of the doshas through personalized diet, lifestyle, and herbal remedies in order to promote overall health and well-being. One should always consult a qualified doctor before taking or following anything as a remedy.

Homeopathy

Homeopathy is a system of alternative medicine based on the principle of "like cures like". It was developed in the late 18th century by German physician Samuel Hahnemann.

The central idea behind homeopathy is that a substance that produces symptoms in a healthy person can be used to treat similar symptoms in a sick person. This principle is known as the "law of similars" or "like cures like".

Homeopathic remedies are made from natural substances such as plants, minerals, and animal products. These substances are diluted and succussed (shaken vigorously) to create a potentized remedy that is believed to stimulate the body's natural healing processes.

Homeopathy is a holistic system of medicine, which means that it considers the whole person, including their physical, emotional, and mental state, when selecting a remedy.

Once you get to know about your constitutional remedy (Medicine) it is like hitting two targets with one arrow. You get to know about yourself via the symptoms of that remedy and also whenever you have any health related disturbances, You know exactly what to take which works perfectly and holistically for you.

1. **Mahatma Gandhi:** Gandhi was a strong supporter of homeopathy and used it for himself and his family. He famously said, "Homeopathy cures a greater percentage of cases than any other method of treatment."
2. **Paul McCartney:** The former Beatle has been a longtime advocate for homeopathy and has used it to treat various ailments. He has spoken publicly about his positive experiences with the practice.

Remedies for Acute problems:-

In homeopathy some remedies are for acute problems which have occurred from a short period of time. For these kinds of conditions, the course of treatment is also short.

Constitutional medicine

It is a fundamental concept in homeopathy that refers to the selection of a remedy based on the individual's overall physical, emotional, and mental characteristics. It is believed that every individual has a unique constitutional makeup, and homeopathy aims to match the remedy to the individual's constitutional type.

The constitutional type is determined by a detailed evaluation of the individual's physical, emotional, and mental symptoms, as well as their general characteristics such as temperament, personality traits, and physical attributes. Based on this assessment, a homeopath selects a remedy that best matches the individual's overall constitution, rather than just treating a specific symptom or condition.

The constitutional remedy is intended to stimulate the individual's natural healing ability and restore balance to their entire system, leading to improved health and well-being. Constitutional treatment is typically ongoing and may require adjustments in potency and patterns of intake over time as the individual's symptoms and overall health status change.

I advocate homeopathy for myself until there is some case of emergency. Trust me if some homeopath evaluate your symptoms and personality properly the homeopathic remedy works like a charm.

And if some homeopathic remedy works holistically for you or for anyone else you can get whole insight into physical, mental and emotional characteristics of yours or that person. Because in Homeopathy each medicine has it's own physical, mental and emotional symptoms. If they matches with some individual, the medicine has potential to completely cure that person via the principle of "Like Cures Like" and in that case whole body of an individual get healed rather than a single disease which happens in case of acute remedy.

For Example :- (i) For a person having sulphur as the constitutional remedy.

Sulphur is a constitutional remedy that can be used to treat a wide range of physical, mental, and emotional symptoms.

Some of the sulphur type personalities that have graced our history pages are Albert Einstein, Socrates, Abraham Lincoln, Dr. Samuel Hahnemann (The founder of homeopathy), Carl Gustav Jung, etc.

Some of the common symptoms that indicate the need for Sulphur are:

Physical symptoms:

- Skin problems such as acne, eczema, and psoriasis
- Digestive disorders such as constipation, diarrhea, and bloating

- Respiratory issues such as asthma and bronchitis
- Joint pain and stiffness
- Hot flashes and night sweats
- Chronic fatigue
- Burning sensation in the body
- Offensive body odour

Mental symptoms:

- **Intellectual and philosophical thinking:-** Sulphur personalities tend to be highly intellectual and have a great desire to learn and understand the world around them. They are known for their analytical skills and often have a scientific or philosophical approach to life.
- **A tendency to be disorganized and absent-minded:-** Although they have a great desire to learn and understand, they may have trouble organizing their thoughts and ideas. They tend to be absent-minded and may have difficulty focusing on one task for long periods.
- Overthinking and analyzing things very deeply.
- **Strong desire for independence and freedom:-** Sulphur personalities value their independence and freedom. They are not comfortable with being told what to do and may resist authority.
- Irritability and impatience
- Forgetfulness

Emotional symptoms:

- Deep anxiety and fear

- Depression and melancholy
- Feeling emotionally drained
- Apathy and indifference
- Over-sensitivity to criticism
- Lack of confidence
- Strong sense of creativity and imagination

It is important to note that not everyone who needs Sulphur as a constitutional remedy will exhibit all of these symptoms. The symptoms can vary from person to person, and a trained homeopath will consider the individual's unique symptoms and overall constitution before prescribing Sulphur.

The popularity of homeopathy is increasing once again around the globe due to it's holistic approach and almost zero side effects.

What one should take care of while choosing homeopathy for them is to choose a good doctor who can understand your symptoms properly who can choose an accurate remedy with correct potency for you and there you go, see the magic. Self-medication should not be done.

Although the need for and efficacy of modern medicine have not been denied here, modern medicine, also called allopathic medicine, involves the use of drugs and surgeries to help cure the disease or solve the problem of the patient. After all, the ultimate purpose of any medicine should be to heal and cure.

Samudrik Shastra

Samudrik Shastra, also known as Vedic palmistry or the science of body reading, is an ancient Indian system of knowledge that uses physical features to gain insight into a person's character, personality, and destiny. The system involves the analysis of various physical features, such as the shape of the face, eyes, nose, mouth, hands, feet, and nails, to make predictions about a person's life.

Samudrik Shastra received notable contributions from Hindu sages like Valmiki, Veda Vyasa, Sage Parashara, Varahamihira and Samudrena.

Here are some ways that Samudrik Shastra can help you know yourself better:

1. Hand analysis: In Samudrik Shastra, the hand is analyzed to gain insight into a person's personality and life path. The shape, size, lines, and mounts on the hand are all examined to determine a person's strengths, weaknesses, and potential.

2. Face reading: Samudrik Shastra also involves the analysis of facial features to gain insight into a person's character and destiny. The shape of the face, eyes, nose, and mouth are all examined to determine a person's temperament, emotional nature, and potential for success.

3. Nails analysis: The shape, texture, and color of nails are studied in Samudrik Shastra to reveal a person's health, temperament, and potential for success.

According to a verse attributed to Varahamihira, Samudrika Shastra studies thirteen attributes of a body. They are

1. Anuka – shape or general appearance of the face
2. Unmana – quantity or volume
3. Kanti – glow
4. Gati – Gait
5. Prakriti – Basic nature
6. Mana – Weight

7. Varna – Complexion
8. Sattwa – essential or steadfast wisdom
9. Sneha – smoothness of the body
10. Samhati – the way the joints are formed
11. Sara – Basic material
12. Swara – the nature note from the throat
13. Kshetra – the division of the mental, practical and basic worlds in the overall personality.
14. Later on, the element of gandha (natural odor) was added to the list to make it a study of fourteen basic parameters to reveal the features of a body.

For example a man with a broad forehead is likely to succeed in the administrative field, a man with a convex forehead is more of a communicator and hence good for a marketing job, and one with a concaving forehead is of reflective temperament and is ideally suited for creative jobs.

It should be taken into care that observing only one feature of someone will not be sufficient to evaluate that person's personality features and predictions about and hence, all the criteria should be considered after proper study.

Samudrik Shastra can be a useful tool for gaining insight into your personality, character, and life path. However, it's important to remember that the interpretation of physical features should always be done with care and sensitivity.

CHAPTER-2

The Energy Thing

Before taking any other chapter in sequence I would love to introduce to you with the energy thing.

Before going to the different laws of Energy Let's give a sight to what the famous personalities have to say about the Law of Energy and it's role in our lives. Some of the examples are:-

1. Albert Einstein - "Everything is energy and that's all there is to it. Match the frequency of the reality you want and you cannot help but get that reality. It can be no other way. This is not philosophy. This is physics."
2. Oprah Winfrey - "I believe that everything is energy. That we are made up of cells that are made up of molecules that are made up of atoms that are made up of energy. We are just a big, pulsating, vibrant mass of energy."
3. Wayne Dyer - "Everything in the universe is energy - including us. And when we tune into that energy, we can attract whatever we want into our lives."
4. Deepak Chopra - "Your body is not a frozen sculpture of the past, but a flowing river of energy and information that is constantly renewing itself."
5. Tony Robbins - "Energy is the essence of life. Every day you decide how you're going to use it by knowing

what you want and what it takes to reach that goal, and by maintaining focus."

All of these famous personalities recognize the importance of energy in our lives, and how it can be harnessed to achieve our goals and live more fulfilling lives. Whether through physics, philosophy, or spirituality, the Law of Energy is a fundamental principle that can help us understand and improve ourselves and our world.

When people talk about the law of energy, most of them only mean the law of attraction by it. The reason behind this is that with time many books have been written on this Universal law. Due to the materialistic approach of the people, they find the law of attraction as their savior and they think it will work like a magic spell. Here, I am not denying the efficacy of the law of attraction. But for something to be applicable for you you must know the principle and logic behind it, how it works? What are the other laws associated with it.

So Let us now talk about some of the laws and Universe and philosophies on which these laws are based so that we can understand the energy thing in depth and in this way it will be more fruitful for you in much easier way.

So basically the Law of attraction is one of the law among the 12 intrinsic and unchanging laws of the Universe that ancient cultures have always intuitively known.

These are often seen connected to **Hermetic Philosophy** of Ancient Egypt and the Hawaiian Technique of Meditation Called **Ho'oponopono**. Now, let's first talk about The Hermetic Philosophy.

The Hermetic Philosophy:-

Hermetic philosophy is a spiritual and philosophical tradition that originated in ancient Egypt and later developed in Greece during the Hellenistic period (323 BC – 32 BC). It is based on a set of writings known as the Corpus Hermeticum, which are attributed to the mythical figure Hermes Trismegistus.

The surviving writings of Hermeticism are known as the *Corpus Hermetica*, which is composed of a series of letters from a master, Hermes Trismegistus, wherein he tries to enlighten his disciple. These letters were lost to the western world after classical times, but survived in the Byzantine (Eastern Roman Empire) libraries. In the Fifteenth century, the letters were rediscovered and translated into Latin.

What are the 7 Hermetic Principles?

The principles of Hermetic philosophy include:

1. **The Principle of Mentalism: -**
   The All is mind; The Universe is Mental.
   This principle states that the universe is mental in nature, and that everything in the physical world is a manifestation of the universal mind. When we recognize how much our thoughts manifest every day, we see that when we can control our mind, we control our lives. We can get better at this through spiritual practices such as meditation, which help us train the mind and also by living consciously having a watch on the mind.

2. **The Principle of Correspondence: -**
   As above, so below; as below, so above. As within, so without; as without, so within.
   This principle says that there is a correspondence between the physical and spiritual realms, and that the

laws and principles that govern one realm also apply to the other. For eg.- The micro is in the macro, and vice versa.

It's closely related to the first principle of mentalism and states that what we hold in our thoughts and mind will become our reality. It explains the many planes of existence, including those of lower and higher vibrational frequencies and how they're connected.

3. **The Principle of Vibration:-**

   Nothing rests; Everything moves; Everything vibrates.

   This principle states that everything in the universe is in a constant state of vibration, and that these vibrations create different levels of manifestation.

   The idea of "vibes" is not very new but it has been around for a long, long time. You may have often felt when your vibes matches with others' you feel very friendly and comfortable around them. The principle of vibration states that all things, both physical matter and spiritual energy, hold a certain vibration. Even on different emotional state our heart produces different vibrations.

   Basic science states that atoms are in constant motion, as is the universe itself. With this principle, we acknowledge that we have the power to control our vibration rather than our vibration controlling us. You might be noticing all of these principles are deeply interwoven and connected.

4. **The Principle of Polarity:-**

   Everything is dual; Everything has poles; Everything has its pair of opposites; Like and unlike are the same; Opposites are identical in nature, but different in degree; Extremes meet; All truths, are but half-truths; All paradoxes may be reconciled.

   This principle states that everything in the universe has an opposite, and that these opposites are necessary for the manifestation of creation. For E.g.- Love and hate are two ways of experiencing the same thing, a relationship toward something. This is the foundation of alchemy, or the ability to "transmute" your experiences at will. However, Applicating the Polarity principle takes a degree of mental stamina and involves shifting the way you look at something. Any time if a lower vibrational emotion is bringing you down, recognize it, feel it, and transmute it to a more positive one because the thing is same it's just dual. So, shift to the more positive one.

5. **The Principle of Rhythm:-**

   "Everything flows, out and in; everything has its tides; all things rise and fall; the pendulum-swing manifests in everything; the measure of the swing to the right is the measure of the swing to the left; rhythm compensates."

   This principle states that everything in the universe moves in a cyclical pattern, and that these cycles create the rhythms of life. Between the opposite poles of the principle of Polarity, is the pendulum swing of The principle of Rhythm, swinging backward and forward, Never stopping, always changing.

When you are in tune with the Principle of Rhythm and understand that every mental state exists in Rhythm, you can learn to use this principle to your advantage by polarizing yourself to the degree you desire. Then, through awareness of this principle and how it manifests, holding yourself there to keep the pendulum from swinging you backwards to its extreme. Just a sense of awareness towards self and knowing of the principle is enough to applicate it.

6. **The Principle of Cause and Effect:-**

   Every cause has its effect; Every effect has its cause; Everything happens according to law, 'Chance is but a name for law not recognized' There are many planes of causation, but nothing escapes the law.

   This principle states that every action has a corresponding reaction, and that all things are interconnected and influence each other. Meaning, that nothing merely 'happens for no reason,' and that there is no such thing as 'chance.'

   When something doesn't go as planned or you find yourself unhappy, ask yourself about the cause? When we take action to get the result we want, we move from feeling like a victim to feeling empowered and happier than before.

7. **The Principle of Gender:-**

   Gender is in everything; Everything has its masculine and feminine principles; Gender manifests on all planes.

This principle states that everything in the universe has both masculine and feminine aspects, and that these aspects work together to create balance and harmony. This means that the masculine and feminine exist not only in the physical plane, but also in the mental, and the spiritual as well.

The masculine represents assertive, progressive, conquesting, penetrative, explorative energy that drives progress. The feminine is the receptive, sacred, treasured, protective energy, that maintains tradition and honors the priority of what is most important, while nourishing that which is most essential to life. The unity of these two energies is essential for creation, and when one has a balance of both, they're better able to apply all of the principles together for maximum benefit.

Accept all the parts of yourself, and understand that balance in all is key for self-mastery. Buddha called this the middle way, and it's all about the balance of masculine and feminine; of heavenly and Earthbound; and of the mind, body, and spirit. When we can achieve this balance within ourselves, we're well equipped to harness all of these principles and use them in our lives for good.

At the last of hermeticism these all principles may sound like a lot to you. But you need to understand that these principles run at very deeper level and with great connection with each other, completely woven. It may take a long time to fully understand and embody them and with time you will get to know many new aspects and deeper levels and slowly it will come into habit to become part of life. So, understand, Read, Act and practice them more in order to master your mind and your life for betterment.

The 12 Laws of The Universe :-

The 12 Laws of the universe describe the way things operate in this time space reality. The 12 Universal Laws are known to be originated from the source or you say it God, The Universe or higher Energy, etc.

Just like the Physical laws of the Science, for e.g. The law of Gravity, these Universal laws were not invented like Gravity was always there, it's just that Newton discovered it through observation and experiences. In the same way these universal laws were not invented but they already exists as the part of the existence and we got to know about them through their observation and experience.

The interesting fact is that they always work, whether you are aware of them or not. Understanding the laws of the universe puts you at advantage not just only to survive but to thrive in the universe.

Although, there are many laws of universe (some even unnamed) that works on different given moments but there is a total of 12 laws of universe that are universally accepted to be true. Among them the law of divine oneness is said to be the main law of universe which states that at spiritual level we are never separated from god or from each other and hence it brings peace to our mind by making us aware of being in oneness with the source, The universe, the highest energy or you can say god.

Now let us know about the 12 laws of the Universe one by one. Among these Universal laws more than one law show resemblance with the 7 hermetic principles.

1. Law of Divine Oneness :-

Law of Divine Oneness, so profound,
States everything in the universe is bound.
Connected we are, one at the core,
Vibrating at frequencies, like never before.
Compassion and acceptance, the key,
To embrace those we don't fully see.
Uniting thought, we all are one,
Connected at the core, until our time is done.

The most foundational and main law of universe states that everything is connected and the whole universe follows oneness. Nothing is separate at spiritual level and is just an extension of the Source, which gives us the uniting thought that we all are one at the energy level and the only difference is that we are vibrating at certain different frequencies.

This can be practiced exercising compassion and acceptance towards those, whom we don't understand.

2. Law of Vibration:-

Interact with care, watch what you share
Your vibe, don't impair, attract good air
Meditation, a vital preparation
Elevate your vibration, enjoy the sensation

This law states that everything in this world is made up of energy and is vibrating at a specific frequency either it is tangible or intangible.

This means everything that we see and that we don't see like our friend, pet or phone and thoughts, emotions and feelings respectively are comprised of energy and are constantly vibrating.

This also gives a quick hack to use law of attraction to attract your desires into reality, all you need to do is vibrational alignment.

Manifestation becomes quite easier and simple with the help of the law of vibration all we have to do is to identify the vibration of our burning desire and then tuning ourselves to the same vibrations in order to get the favourable manifestation.

That's why it's said that your company matters a lot for whether you will succeed or not because energy is contagious and the people you come in contact with affect your vibrations their words affect your mindset at subconscious level and further your mindset tune yourself to certain vibrations of different frequencies.

By the Law of Attraction, following the principle of "like attracts like" your vibration will attract things, people, situations, experiences, and outcomes with the same vibration into your life. Yoga, meditation, Environment and involvement, etc. along with 'conscious will', are some of the exercises to help you elevate your vibrations. So tune and enjoy.

3. Law of Correspondence:-

In the symphony of life, tune in to your vibration,
Find the faults, make corrections, feel your elation.
Chaotic or peaceful, it's all within your station,
Conscious living can bring a transformation.

It states that your internal state reflects directly as the external reality of your life.

Hence this law works as the assessment of your vibrational alignment.

If you feel contented and grateful for your life that means you are in alignment and harmony with the vibrations of your desired reality and hence you are in alignment with the loving energy of the universe.

If your life seems out of order and you feel discontented, anxious, stressful and something is missing out of it then you should check the fault in your tuning. Once you identifies them work towards vibrations of different and desired outcomes.

Final words are that if someone's life is fearful and chaotic that's because there is chaos and fear inside that person and if life seems peaceful and lovely that's because there's peace and love within that person. What you create within is what you manifest outside. Conscious living can help to the troubled individuals.

4. Law of Attraction:-

Law of Attraction, hold on tight,
Manifest your dreams with all your might,
Don't let uncertainty cloud your sight,
Stay positive, keep your vibes light.
Trust the universe, everything will be right,
To all my dreamers, I wish you a future bright.
"Like Attracts like",

It states that your energy is attracting situations, events, and experiences that are a direct match for your energy.

Undoubtedly the most talked about universal law and the most often used law for manifestation. It says that like attracts like and you get what you focus on without any doubt. Yes, it's very important to not having any possible doubt about the happening of the desired outcome. Just having pure faith and belief of getting what is asked or desired.

Miracle happens to those who believe in their happening, just like a kid believe in the abundance of the universe or you can say god. For what is impossible for the source itself?. Don't use logics , because magic is called a magic because it has no logic to define it's happening.

Don't ask how?

Don't ask when?

Avoid yourself from asking and craving too much because that too will send the vibrations of desperation and what you give here is what you get back from the universe.

Remember one thing, universe is mental and it records your vibrations as per your thoughts, action and emotional priorities and send them back to you in a magnified form, whether good or bad, whether favourable or unfavourable.

Universe doesn't differentiate between good or bad because universe follows the principle of polarity. Whether it's good or bad for you, for universe, like and unlike are the same; Opposites are identical in nature with different degrees. Universe follows you blindly without imposing it's definitions of good and bad on you.

For example if you want love, send the vibrations of love into the universe with belief and you will get a lots of love back.

It all comes down to your energy. Your energy is constantly attracting situations, events, and experiences that are a direct match for your energy.

In other words you don't get what you want but you get what you are and what you believe you truly deserve and ask for it firmly with complete faith from the universe as if it is your right.

By applying the Law of Attraction to your own life, you will have absolute clarity over why situations occur the way they do and more importantly, what you can do to shift your energy and change the outcomes you receive.

Once again, too much attachment to the outcome and desperately wanting something will add the uncertainty factor into your mind and more desperation will arise, universe will record it as your priority and will get back to you with making you more and more desperate about the desired outcome. Goodluck to my dreamers.

5. Law of Inspired Action:-

**When we let go of control and
allow ourselves some grace,**

We open up to new paths and find our own pace.

**The real inspiration lies within,
not what we see on the shelf,**

It's about connecting with our true self.

Have you ever practiced being quiet and slowed down? and then suddenly you get answer to a problem or any good inspiration or a creative idea or thought. Ever wondered, How does that happen? The simple logic behind the concept is "Nature Abhors a vacuum" a phrase coined by Aristotle. Which means when we become quite from inside out, we get more aligned with who we really are, as the Law of Divine oneness states- an extension of the source and in that state we get the real inspiration from the within, the inspiration which is truly meant for us.

In other words mental and emotional turbulence hinders our connection with our own true self and hence with the source. Getting slowed down and quiet for some paces creates space for internal guidance. The urge to control the happening of the things and situations and the want for the certainty of the desired results shut the way to new possibilities. Rather, being open to all possibilities makes room for new ways of achieving the goals and make us able to explore our greatest purpose in life.

6. Law of Perpetual Transmutation of Energy:-

**With every thought and action, we create a reaction,
Shifting our energy towards positive or
negative attraction.
To uplift our vibration, it's our job to take action,
Responding with positivity, not impulsively
in every situation.**

The words themselves define the law as "Constant Transformation or Fluctuation of Energy". This law advocates the prior laws like Law of Vibration and The law of Attraction which respectively states that everything is energy and like attracts like. Your energy is always shifting or fluctuating either toward higher vibration that is positively or Lower vibration that is negatively based on our thoughts, actions and our reactions to certain actions. Now our thoughts and actions are the drivers of the shift of energy for us. So it's our duty to channelize our thoughts and vibrations and uplift our energy with the help of our positive thoughts and actions and also by learning how to respond positively rather than reacting impulsively.

7. Law of Cause and Effect:-

Our thoughts, our words, and our actions in harmonic vibration,

Sending signals to the universe, creating a ripple sensation.

The energy we put out will come back in kind,

So let's be mindful of what we send, for it will affect our mind.

You can understand this law better by recalling the third law of newton that is "Every action has an equal and opposite reaction". Now here, Opposite doesn't means opposite in nature but it means opposite direction, for eg.- pushing the water backward makes the boat move forward. In this case push of certain force is the action and the push of the same force and intensity in the opposite direction is the reaction. Likewise, our thoughts, our words and our actions , these all produce certain vibrations and we often unconsciously send them to universe. Universe in turn records the sent vibrations and send them back in the form of reaction or similar realities. It doesn't mean what we put out there in universe come back to us at the moment but those energy vibrations will have ripple effect and we eventually be affected by it in the form of same results and realities. So we need to remember that for every cause there is an effect and we should think and act accordingly.

8. Law of Compensation:- This law simply states,

"What You Reap is What You Sow"

Or

What you give to others shall be given to you

Or

What you without from others shall be withheld from you

Or

Future consequences of experiences and reality are inevitably shaped by present Thoughts and Actions.

Some people often feel like they are not loved, not praised or not liked by others. Then they should look at themselves that how they treat others. Sometimes people expect only good behaviour from others even after providing them with the bad one. But they need to understand that this works both ways. If you can't love someone then you shouldn't also hate them. Because love can't be expected in return of hatred in the same way Praise can't be expected in return of unfair criticism and jealousy. Either remain constant or treat others with good behavior and pure emotions in order to get the same.

Whenever you express or have negative emotions regarding someone this not only show up and affect at physical level but also at the energy level. Your energies reach the person before you words and your actions. If you feel that you really have accumulated lot of negative emotions for someone and to someone, in that case you can practice ho'oponopono technique. It works magically for energy cleansing and Law of attraction applications. We will talk about this technique later in this book

9. Law of Relativity:-

Life's journey is indeed quite inventive,
Teaching us truths that are all relative.
Connect to your heart and evolve higher,
Inferior or superior, it's just ego's fire.
True self-esteem and humility as one,
In essence, we're all equal under the sun.

Everything is neutral in reality the difference is that we all have our own perspective and perception of what that reality means to us. Relativism exists in all things. This law explains why two people have entirely different experiences instead of going through the same situations. For e.g.- if we are ungrateful and unhappy for some situation let's say living standards, it could be because it's our perception due to comparison with someone else's. This law makes us feel grounded the most. This law states that each person receive a series of problems for the purpose of the strengthening the light within and there is always someone else who is having it worse than us. The law of relativity shows us that it all really is relative. This law grounds us and teaches us to connect to our heart while solving the set of problems received as the process of evolution to a higher self. As Eckhart Tolle, in his book, A New Earth, writes, "In form, you are and will always be inferior to some; superior to others. In essence, you are neither inferior nor superior to anyone. True self-esteem and true humility arise out of that realization. In the eyes of the ego, self-esteem and humility are contradictory. In truth, they are one and the same."

10. Law of Polarity:-

In life's dance, opposites prance,
Like and unlike, in a cosmic trance,
Dualities meet, extremes greet,
All truths are but a half-sweet.
Keep in mind, the opposite you'll find,
A positive pole of a different kind,
Manifest the good, let go of the bad,
Reconcile paradoxes, make your soul glad.

"Yin and Yang" this Chinese philosophical concept is the first thing which came into my mind while writing about this law of universe, which describes opposite but interconnected forces. The law of polarity validates that this is a universe of duality. It states that everything in life has an opposite. There is a solution for every problem and opportunity for every obstacle. It gives us the hope and zeal to change the worse part of our life to their best, because we know that the complete opposite of what you take as the worse exists as the best and just only need to be manifested with the help of other laws of nature. To get more insight, you should consider these lines of Napoleon Hill, Author of the classic, Think And Grow Rich, "Every adversity, every failure and every heartache carries with it the seed of an equivalent or a greater benefit." The Kybalion, an ancient book published in and around 1808, by a group of unidentified initiates, "Everything is dual; everything has poles; everything has its pair of opposites; like and unlike are the same; opposites are identical in nature, but different in degree;

extremes meet; all truths are but half-truths; all paradoxes may be reconciled."

So, whichever situation or obstacle you are in? You should always keep in mind that the exactly opposite and positive pole of the situation exists and just need to be manifested. So, tune into what the opposite looks like.

I wish you luck!

11. Law of Rhythm:-

Embrace the hard times, they won't last,
In the end, you'll come out strong and fast.
Every low is a chance to grow,
Find joy in the journey, let it show.
Remember, tough roads lead to bright days,
Stay positive in all your ways.

The Law of Rhythm refers to the idea that everything in the universe moves in a cyclical pattern, from the rise and fall of the tides to the ebb and flow (a recurrent pattern of coming and going or decline and regrowth) of our own lives. For example look at the different phases of the moon and your breathe (inhaling and exhaling).

Everything in the universe is moving, flowing, and swinging back and forth in a dance. Either developing or dying, that is the creational cycle. In life, economy, and relationships, a high era is usually followed by a low one. It abides by the universal law. Everything is governed by it, including our health. It just indicates that you should slow down, take a break, and observe and analyze during this lull or lean moment. Understanding this law can help us navigate the ups and downs of life with greater ease and acceptance.

So next time you hit a low in some expect of life, look at it with ease with a satisfying conscious thought in mind that it too will pass and the positive side will appear soon, and after all, it is only the low phase of life that teaches us the strength. So, embrace the difficult times and know that they are shaping you into a stronger person. Always remember to find joy in the journey, even when the road gets tough. Wish you Joy!

12. Law of Gender:-

**Emotions, creativity, spirituality,
all in the divine feminine shine,
The masculine energy, with traits like authority
and confidence align,
Neither is superior, both must intertwine,
For answers to benefit, in harmony they must combine,
In a world where male traits often take the lead,
Reconnecting with our feminine side is what we need.**

According to the Law of Gender, life functions best when your divine feminine and masculine energies are in harmony. The aspect of our consciousness that links us to traits like intuition, feeling, emotions, creativity, and spirituality is represented by the divine feminine. The divine masculine energy, which links us to traits like reasoning, authority, confidence, objectivity, and action-taking, is the exact opposite of this feminine energy. It's important to remember that one is not superior than the other. To develop answers for the utmost benefit, the divine masculine and feminine must coexist peacefully. Yet historically, society has valued male traits above feminine ones.

Hence, we must reestablish contact with our divine feminine in order to restore balance to our lives.

The most talked about one is the law of attraction, but what about the laws of polarity, spiritual oneness, or correspondence? The law of attraction is simply one of the 12 universal principles, and learning the other 11 may help us live life that is more align with our spiritual selves.

These principles are believed to be the foundation of the universe, and understanding and applying them can lead to a more fulfilling and harmonious life. By incorporating these principles into our daily lives, we can achieve greater balance, peace, and abundance.

Let's now discuss "The Law of Attraction," which is the most often mentioned, discussed, and largely acknowledged of the 12 known laws of the universe.

The Law of Attraction (LOA)

Before taking a deep dive into the law of attraction, let's have a look at the words of some well-known personalities.

Several well-known people have discussed the Law of Energy and how it affects our daily lives. Here are a few examples:

- Buddha - "All that we are is the result of what we have thought."
- Albert Einstein - "Everything is energy and that's all there is to it. Match the frequency of the reality you want and you cannot help but get that reality. It can be no other way. This is not philosophy. This is physics."
- Nikola Tesla - "If you want to find the secrets of the Universe, think in terms of energy, frequency and vibration."

- Oprah Winfrey - "I believe that everything is energy. That we are made up of cells that are made up of molecules that are made up of atoms that are made up of energy. We are just a big, pulsating, vibrant mass of energy."
- Wayne Dyer - "Everything in the universe is energy - including us. And when we tune into that energy, we can attract whatever we want into our lives."
- Tony Robbins - "Energy is the essence of life. Every day you decide how you're going to use it by knowing what you want and what it takes to reach that goal, and by maintaining focus."
- Oprah Winfrey - "You become what you believe. You are where you are today in your life based on everything you have believed."
- Will Smith - "The first step before anyone else in the world believes it is that you have to believe it."
- Rhonda Byrne - "The law of attraction is the law of creation. Quantum physicists tell us that the entire Universe emerged from thought!"
- Wayne Dyer - "Your thoughts and feelings together create an 'energetic fingerprint' that magnetizes the people, circumstances and events into your life."
- Marcus Aurelius Antoninus - "The universe is change; our life is what our thoughts make it."
- Ramtha - "To let life happen to you is irresponsible. To create your day is your divine right."
- Napoleon Hill - "What the mind of man can conceive and believe, the mind of man can achieve."
- Abraham Hicks – The entire universe is conspiring to give you everything that you want.

- Dr. Robert Schuller - "You are what you think about all day long."
- Albert Einstein - "I admit thoughts influence the body."
- Michael Bernard Beckwith - It has been proven now scientifically that an affirmative thought is hundreds of times more powerful than a negative thought."
- Anthony Robbins - "If you do what you've always done, you'll get what you've always gotten."
- Robert Kiyosaki - "Your future is created by what you do today, not tomorrow."

One of the most crucial foundations of the law of attraction is belief, and as humans, we have a tendency to believe something passionately when we hear others express their support and admiration for it. I suppose the ideas expressed by some notable individuals up there have strengthened your belief in the law of attraction. Although it's not always reliable or necessary to accept what celebrities say but if a lot of them are saying the same thing, then there must be something to take into account.

So let's get into that something, called as Law of Attraction.

Concepts related to LOA

Like Attracts Like:-

If I had to define the law of attraction in one sentence I would say it's a universal law which works on the concept of "Like attracts Like".

However, It may seem simple to use the law of attraction to bring your aspirations to life, but doing so requires careful thoughts, deliberate actions, and a sense of surrender. Even if we're not aware of it, we constantly "attract" either positive or negative energy depending on the energy we are putting forth.

We are all like magnets, reflecting and drawing to us whatever is in our minds because, after all, "like attracts like".

Nature abhors a vacuum:-

Aristotle coined the phrase "nature abhors a vacuum," According to this theory, no space in nature can really exist as empty; something must constantly occupy it. It's crucial to eliminate negativity from your life in order to create room for good transformation.

It implies that by getting rid of the bad things in your life, you may create room for more good things to enter. This philosophy is often applied in the context of decluttering bad habits, negative thought patterns, cutting toxic relationships and negative mindset and along with it following positive mindset will provide our life with more positivity, beauty and contentment.

The present is always perfect:-

It teaches us that there will always be reasons to be unhappy if you look for them, but finding solutions to problems is crucial to change your reality, so that you can attracts the things you want. It's not like that you won't notice negativity or won't have negative thoughts and feelings because that's a natural process and can only be conquered with practice and time. In the present moment focus on improving the bad circumstances as much as you can because that is what you really have in your hand, the present moment, and your actions in it and reactions towards it.

By focusing on what you can really control and taking action towards improving it, you'll feel more empowered and less overwhelmed by negativity. Remember, it's not about ignoring your emotions but rather finding a healthy way to deal with them and having an optimistic and positive approach towards any situation so that the future outcomes will be more harmonious and favourable.

The rule emphasizes the notion that you should concentrate your efforts on figuring out how to deal the current circumstance the best. It is ultimately your option as to how you think, behave, and what occurs to you, as opposed to feeling annoyed or dissatisfied. Therefore, it's important to practice mindfulness and self-awareness to identify and manage negative thoughts and emotions. This can help attract positive experiences and emotions into your life. Because at last what all we have is "The Present Moment". Good Luck! My Warriors, I wish you joy.

As we know that law of attraction is a game of energy and energy operates at very subtle level. To applicate the law of attraction in our favour or for desirable outcomes we must understand every microscopic aspect of it's working, why it fails to work for people? Precautions while practicing, etc.

The law of attraction has seven subsidiary laws. There are some valuable pearls in this list, even if we don't view any of them to be natural laws. But off course they are subparts of the natural law itself that is the law of attraction.

So let's dive some deeper into sub parts of the Law of Attraction:-

Subparts of the Law of Attraction

1. **The Law of Manifestation:** This sub-law counsels us to direct our attention and effort on the present in order to influence it. Worrying about the past or the future does not bring about change. Yet if we work hard today,

we can build a brighter future and accomplish our aspirations.

According to the Law of Manifestation, our thoughts and emotions shape our reality, thus whatever we concentrate on will come to pass in our life. Affirmations based on the Law of Attraction are a powerful tool for helping you concentrate on what you want instead of what you don't want in order to manifest the life you desire.

2. **The Law of Magnetism:** It is stated in this sub-law that like attracts like. Positive thoughts ultimately attract positive ideas, whereas negative thoughts would do so of their own accord. If all we do is keep thinking negatively, unpleasant events will continue happening to us. According to the Law of Magnetism, the people, things, and opportunities that have entered your life as well as the situations in which you have found yourself are all a direct outcome of the energy you have sent into the universe.

But still, if we look for the good in life, our emphasis will be more on discovering positive chances and experiences, which leads to enhancing our well-being.

You attract what you are, not what you want, Yes you heard it right. Now read that again. We'll talk more about this later in this chapter.

3. **The Law of Unwavering Desire:** This sub-law is all about maintaining our concentration on the ambitions and objectives that would enhance our life. Our health, professional success, and interpersonal relationships all improve when we have clear, optimistic expectations. We may go through a lot of changes as we go through life. To remain grounded, though, we must be aware of

how we really feel about our beliefs and objectives. And although our beliefs or wants may change over the course of our life, having a strong sense of who we are will help us stay committed to achieving our most important objectives.

Hence, In order for you to attract or accomplish anything in your life, your desire must be unwavering and powerful. Your desires won't be able to attract what you want if they are feeble and lack a rock-solid base.

4. **The Law of Delicate Balance :** The equilibrium between the many forces and components makes up the cosmos. We need equilibrium since we are little universes within ourselves. True happiness and contentment can only be felt when all the dimensions of your life are in harmony. Yet in order to create balance, thankfulness and acceptance are necessary.

There might be good days and bad days. Once in a while, you can face failure or a setback. The truth is that it is a fact of life. Accepting our shortcomings is beneficial since they provide a chance to grow. We must acknowledge our losses in the same way that we appreciate our victories. That's how we can maintain a delicate balance in our lives.

Because if we give to much emphasis to lows in life we will ultimately attract the same consequences, we can avoid it by accepting these as the part of life and in case of giving too much emphasis on highs in life people either create a sense of insecurity or Ego which are again negative traits to be followed and slowly degrade your positive vibes unknowingly (can be balanced with the help of gratitude and being grounded). You can also look at "The Middle Path" explained by Buddha to get into the deeper dimensions of it.

13. The Law of Harmony:-

The Law of Harmony is a symphony divine, A balance of forces that make life shine.
In tune with the universe, you'll feel alive, Swimming with the current, effortlessly thrive.
Align yourself with nature's flow, Let it guide you where you need to go.
Find peace and fulfillment in harmony's embrace, And live a life full of joy and grace.

The Law of Harmony suggests that when we align ourselves with the natural flow of the universe, life becomes effortless and enjoyable. It emphasises the importance of being in tune with the forces and elements that surround us, and allowing them to guide us towards our goals and desires. By embracing harmony, we can experience a greater sense of peace, fulfilment, and overall well-being. Now you must be thinking how to exactly do it?

So to be in harmony with the natural flow, it is important to let go of resistance and control. Instead, we should trust the universe and allow it to guide us towards our goals. This means being open to new experiences and opportunities, and embracing change rather than fearing . We should also practice mindfulness and self-awareness, tuning into our intuition and inner guidance to make decisions that align with our true selves. By living in harmony with the universe, we can cultivate a sense of balance and peace in our lives.

I wish harmony and joy to my lovely readers.

14. The Law of Right Action:-

The Law of Right Action, it's true, Your words and deeds affect me and you.
How you treat others echoes back, And determines the quality of your life's track.
Be kind to others and act with care, For this positivity will fill the air.
Focus on right action day by day, And blessings will come along the way.

According to the Law of Right Action, the quality of your experiences in life is determined by your words and deeds, which have an impact on the environment around you. The way you act and treat others will affect how you get treated?

The Law of Right Action emphasizes the importance of being mindful of our actions and treating others with kindness and respect. This also means taking responsibility for our actions and the impact they have on others. We cannot control how others behave towards us, but we can control how we react and respond to their actions. By choosing to respond with kindness and compassion, even in difficult situations, we can break the cycle of negativity and create a more peaceful and harmonious environment. Along with it, practicing right action can also improve our own well-being and provide us with inner peace.

This law is not just limited to our interactions with other people, but also applies to our relationship with the environment and the world at large. Our actions have an impact on the planet, and it is our responsibility to act in a way that is sustainable and respectful to the earth. By being mindful of our consumption habits and reducing our carbon footprint, we can contribute to the greater good of society and the world. The Law of Right Action reminds us that we are all interconnected and our actions have a ripple effect that extends beyond our immediate surroundings. Therefore, it is important to act with intention and thoughtfulness.

After all, we will eventually be treated in accordance with how we treat others.

15. The Law of Universal Influence:-

Look up at night and see,
How the stars twinkle with glee,
We may feel small and weak,
But our impact is what we should seek.
Every thought and action we make,
Becomes a part of the Universe's sake,
It's vital to stay aware, To control our energy's flare.
Listen closely to the signs,
From the Universe's designs,
Follow your dreams without fear,
And spread positivity everywhere!

Never underestimate the power of your thoughts and actions. You are not just a mere speck in the grand scheme of things. You are an important piece of the puzzle, and your contribution matters. Embrace your uniqueness and use it to make a positive impact on the world around you. Remember, you are a part of the Universe, and the Universe is a part of you.

Our energy and it's vibrations are interconnected with the Universe, and our thoughts and actions have a significant impact on the world. We should embrace our uniqueness and use it to make a positive impact, while being aware of our thoughts, feelings, and actions, and paying attention to signs from the Universe. By doing so, we can effectively control our energy and increase our positive impact on the world.

Therefore, it's crucial to take the time to clarify your goals and ensure that they align with your values and aspirations. This will help you stay focused, motivated, and committed to achieving the outcomes you desire. Don't be afraid to revisit and revise your goals as needed, as this can help you stay on track and make meaningful progress towards your dreams. Remember, a clear vision leads to clear results as compared to the vague or uncertain goals which will only lead to unclear outcomes. By being direct and specific, you increase the likelihood of achieving the results you desire. So take the time to define and refine your goals to achieve the success you deserve.

After learning about the subparts of the Law of Attraction let's now move to the key points which works as the foundation stones while practicing law of attraction.

Understanding the Key Components of the LOA :-

❖ **Thoughts :-**

> *The Law of Attraction, what a sensation,*
> *Our thoughts have immense creation,*
> *Be careful of what you meditate,*
> *For similar outcomes will be your fate.*

Imagine a world where your thoughts have the power to manifest into reality. That's what The Law of Attraction proposes - your vibes attract your tribe! It's like a cosmic game of "what you think is what you get." From attracting good vibes to somber ones, your inner voice shapes the course of your fate. So, be mindful of your thoughts because they spell out the blueprint to life's outcomes!

For instance, if someone constantly thinks about how they never have enough money and feel anxious about their financial situation, they may continue to attract financial struggles. On the other hand, if someone focuses on abundance and gratitude for what they have, they may attract more opportunities for financial success.

❖ Beliefs:-

> *Our beliefs, oh so grand,*
> *Tie us close to thoughts in hand,*
> *Shaping all we see and feel,*
> *Helping our experiences to heal.*
> *Bringing positivity to our lives,*
> *Attracting good, as dreams revive.*

Belief in the law of attraction is crucial in this process, as it helps to manifest the desired outcome and keep one motivated during the challenging journey of shifting limiting beliefs. It is essential to hold onto the belief that our thoughts and emotions have immense power in shaping our reality, and by cultivating positive beliefs and attitudes, we can attract abundance and success into our lives.

For example, a person who believes they will never find love may struggle to attract healthy relationships. By shifting this belief to one of abundance and trust in the universe, they may attract a loving partner and cultivate a fulfilling romantic relationship. Through the practice of gratitude and positive affirmations, they can continue to manifest positive experiences and ultimately create the joyful life they desire.

❖ Emotions:-

The Law of Attraction, it's clear to see
Emotions play a big part, that's the key
Joy, gratitude, and love, they make us shine
Attracting positivity, all the time!

it is important to be mindful of our thoughts and emotions and to choose to focus on the positive aspects of our lives. When we consciously choose to cultivate positive emotions, we are sending out a powerful signal to the universe that we are ready to receive more abundance, joy, and love.

On the other hand, when we experience negative emotions such as anger, fear, and sadness, we lower our vibrational frequency and attract more negativity. This is why it's important to be aware of our emotions and make a conscious effort to shift them towards positivity. One way to do this is through gratitude practices, such as writing down things we're thankful for each day. Another way is through mindfulness meditation, which can help us observe and detach from negative thoughts and emotions. By raising our vibrational frequency and focusing on positivity, we can attract more abundance and joy into our lives.

This is the essence of the Law of Attraction - like attracts like, and our emotions play a crucial role in this process.

❖ Visualization :-

Visualization is the key, To manifesting what you see.
Imagine yourself in every way, And your dreams will come to stay.
See the outcomes that you require, Close your eyes and just admire.

Let your thoughts and feelings merge, And your desires will soon converge.
By using visualization and it's power, Imagine yourself in that perfect hour.

Visualisation in the law of attraction is a powerful technique that can help you attract the things you want in life. By imagining yourself already having achieved your goals, with the help of visualisation, you can increase your motivation to take action towards them, and with the help of it, you also communicate with the universe about your burning desires, believing as if they are already accomplished in order to make them a reality.

So, if you want to manifest your dreams, close your eyes and visualise yourself already living the life you desire, Feel that happiness, that contentment, and your loved ones celebrating and congratulating you. Go into as much detail as you can.

But remember one thing your heart should completely believe the outcome of visualisation; there should not be a single doubt. If you have a single doubt, work on it, find a way and visualize when you are free from all doubt and feeling comfortable. Don't ask how, or when; just visualise. With practice, you'll be able to use visualisation as a tool to create a beautiful and fulfilling life.

❖ **Action:-**

To manifest your desires, you must take action,
Don't just think positively, that's just a fraction,
Align with your goals, show the universe you care,
Take consistent action, and be aware,
Success and happiness can soon be yours to hold,
Combine thoughts with action, let your dreams unfold.

Taking Action is always crucial for achieving your goals. It is not enough to simply think positively or believe in the power of manifestation. You must also take intentional and consistent steps towards your desired outcome. This could involve researching, planning, practising healthy habits, or seeking out opportunities. By doing so, you are not only aligning yourself with the energy of your desires, but also demonstrating to the universe that you are serious about manifesting them.

By combining positive thoughts with purposeful action, you can harness the power of the Law of Attraction and create the life you want. So, take that first step today and trust that the universe will support you in achieving your dreams.

❖ Acceptance :-

To manifest all that we dream,
Acceptance is the key it would seem.
Good or bad, we must embrace,
And let go of resistance and chase.
Focus on the present, be grateful too,
And positive outcomes will come through.
Let go of negativity and strife,
And attract more positivity in life.
Acceptance doesn't mean giving up on desire,
But trusting the universe's plan to transpire.
Combine it with visualisation and action,
To fasten manifestation's reaction.

Accepting both good and bad is the very first step towards moving ahead in life and manifesting the life of our dreams. By accepting the present moment and being grateful for what we have, we can shift our focus towards the things we want to manifest. Instead of dwelling on negative experiences or outcomes, we can choose to focus on the positive and attract more of it into our lives. Acceptance also helps us let go of resistance and attachment, allowing us to trust in the universe and its plan for us.

It's important to remember that acceptance doesn't mean giving up on our dreams or settling for less than we desire. Instead, it means embracing the present moment and trusting that the universe has our best interests at heart. By combining acceptance with positive visualization and action towards our goals works as perfect combination of catalysts which fastens the reaction of manifestation.

And here, acceptance in the case of positive outcomes is equally important. Sometimes people start to get what they desire, but from inside they don't accept themselves as worthy of getting it, and eventually, they end up losing it.

❖ Forgiveness :-

Let go of burdens, it's plain to see,
To reach your goals, set yourself free.
Forgive and move on, let anger expire,
Focus on your dreams, light the fire.
Negativity blocks the law of attraction,
Positive energy, the key to satisfaction.
Contentment can't be felt with negativity inside,
Let go, forgive, and enjoy life's ride.

Your baggage should be as minimal as possible in order to reach the top. In other words, it is important to let go of unnecessary burdens and distractions in order to focus on achieving your goals and reaching your full potential. By minimising your baggage, you can lighten your load and move forward with greater ease and clarity.

Forgiveness after acceptance does exactly the same for you. It helps you relieve the burdens of anger, jealousy, resentment, and unfavourable events. So that you can invest all your energy in your goal and the steps required to accomplish it.

The law of attraction is an energy game, and until you are filled with the negative emotions, contentment can't be attained. On one hand, they will cost you time and energy, and on the other, you won't be able to focus on the positive emotions and actions required to manifest the life you desire. Contentment can't be experienced until there is any type of negativity inside us.

❖ Gratitude:-

Gratitude is the key, To a life full of glee.
When we focus on what's lack,
We attract more of that.
But when we express our thanks,
Our life becomes a beautiful rank.
The law of attraction responds to our emotion,
Gratitude can bring us more devotion.
It can change our relationships for the best,
And even improve our emotional nest.
So, make gratitude your daily habit,
And watch your life become ever so magic.

Gratitude is an essential element in the law of attraction. By expressing gratitude for what we already have, we express to universe about our true interests and desires in reply of which universe creates same circumstances and results for ourselves.

Gratitude shifts our perspective from one of lack to one of abundance. When we focus on what we don't have, we attract more of the same. But when we express gratitude for what we do have, we attract more abundance and positivity. This is because the law of attraction responds to our thoughts and emotions, and gratitude is a powerful emotion that can attract more of what we desire. In addition, expressing gratitude can also improve our relationships and increase our overall well-being. It can help us to appreciate the people and experiences in our lives and lead to more fulfilling and meaningful connections.

Practising gratitude on a daily basis helps to shift our mindset towards an abundance mentality and strengthens our ability to attract what we desire. By cultivating a grateful mindset, we can attract more abundance, love, and happiness into our lives.

Common hindrances while practicing Law of Attraction:-

- **Limiting Beliefs:-**

What part do limiting beliefs play? Negative or self-limiting beliefs can make using the Law of Attraction much less effective because they get in the way of people getting what they want. Most of the time, these negative beliefs come from bad events in the past, social conditioning, or doubts about oneself. One way to get past these problems is to become more self-aware and figure out what limiting ideas are stopping them. People can question these beliefs by replacing them with positive affirmations and visualizations.

This will gradually change their subconscious mind so that it works with the Law of Attraction. Seeking support from people who share your beliefs or working with a guide can also help you get past limiting beliefs by giving you direction and holding you accountable.

- **Lack of clarity in intentions:**

It is important to have clear, specific goals and intentions when applying the Law of Attraction, as vagueness can lead to confusion and inconsistent results. When setting intentions, it is crucial to be as specific as possible. For example, instead of just desiring "more money," it is more effective to envision a specific amount or a particular source of income because more money doesn't hold any specific amount in itself, so be specific, be clear.

This clarity will help align your thoughts and actions towards achieving your desired outcome. Without clear intentions, you may find yourself attracting mixed signals and encountering difficulties in manifesting your desires.

- **Difficulty maintaining a positive mindset:**

This is about the challenge individuals may face in staying positive consistently while practicing the Law of Attraction. Some techniques, such as gratitude practice or affirmations, can help overcome negativity.

Other strategies, such as visualization or meditation, can also contribute to maintaining a positive mindset.

- **Impatience with manifestation timing:**

Impatience can become a hurdle for individuals seeking immediate results through manifestations. Which makes a person desperate and desperation like it is said before, attracts desperation further.

This desperation can lead to making impulsive decisions or taking actions that are not aligned with their true desires. It is important for individuals to understand that manifestation is a journey that requires time, perseverance, and faith. By practicing patience and trust in the process, one can attract their desired outcomes without the negative effects of desperation. Remember, good things come to those who wait and believe in the power of manifestation.

For example, someone may be trying to manifest a new job and become impatient when they do not receive offers within the timeframe they expected. This impatience can lead to desperation, causing them to apply for any other job out of fear and uncertainty which may be of even below their expectation rather than trusting the manifestation process and waiting for the right opportunity to come along.

Ultimately, their desperation may only attract more desperate situations, prolonging their search for a fulfilling job.

- **Resistance to change:**

Resistance towards change can impact one's ability to align with the energy required for successful manifestation through methods like meditation or visualization exercises that aid in overcoming resistance. It is crucial to acknowledge that resistance to change is a natural response, as humans tend to find comfort in familiarity.

However, embracing change allows individuals to embrace personal growth and open doors to new opportunities. By recognizing and addressing the resistance, one can gradually shift their mindset, making it easier to align their energy with the manifestation process.

Through consistent practice and patience, meditation and visualization exercises, individuals overcome resistance and create positive change and transformations in their lives.

- **Not wanting good for others:**

The people who can't see others achieving or living their dream lives can't get the life of their dreams. No matter how hard they try, because when you accept others living their dream lives and feel happy to see them happy you open ways for yourself to a happy, fulfilling and dream life because you are embracing happiness and joy of others and sending the signals to the universe that you also want a life in which you are happy and contented.

The best takeaways from the author:

- Generally a person has so many desires at a time. When it comes to fulfill them via LOA and Manifestations which requires a lots of powerful and positive vibration and costs you of large amounts of energy and time. Which sometimes makes you exhausted and also you don't have enough time to enjoy the beautiful thing that is life.

- The smart way is to have fewer but wholesome manifestation goals with specific and long term approach. For example saying or journaling the affirmations like " I am grateful for I'm healthy, happy, joyful, contented, guided, blessed and protected, thank you", likewise you can make of your own as per want.

- Always start an affirmation with "I am grateful for" and end with "Thank You", "Thank You God" or "Thank You Universe". Feel and be grateful as has been already provided to you.

- Always say or write your affirmation in present tense as if they have already been manifested.

- The desire to which we give more energy has more chances of manifesting faster into real life. So, this way fewer the desires faster the results. Setting priorities may help here.

- The **golden rule** of manifestation is **Don't ask How?** And **Don't ask When?** Put your logics on side and simply believe in the magic to happen, like a child.
- Desperation will take you nowhere but to further desperation only. So, be balanced in desiring the outcome, middle path of Buddha may help. Don't become too needy and desperate.
- The smartest way possible for a desired life **is to feel being contented whole day long about your HRCM** (Health, Relationship, Career, Money, Etc.) and making affirmations of contentment, which is a simple choice of self. Being contented wholeheartedly opens the doors to opportunities about which we never had thought, imagined and wanted before but surely they are most suited for us or to make us and our life contented.
- Ultimately the universe knows what exactly you know to live a contented life. So feel contented whole day long like a King/Queen, listen to your gut, keep a watch over negative thought patterns and words and limitise them as much as possible.
- There you go to the life you know or may not know is personally designed for you by universe to make you feel contented exactly the way you feel and practice while manifesting.
- Loads of love and good wishes to my readers. May you all live a life full of joy and contentment.

Manifestation with Water technique

Law of attraction with water states that positive or negative thoughts can actually change the molecular structure of water, affecting its properties and overall energy. Most LOA supporters swear by water manifestation as one of the most effective and simple manifestation methods. The core concept of it is founded on the principle that you will attract back the same energy that you radiate. This unusual approach is saying or thinking about your affirmations before a glass or water bottle before drinking it.

In an experiment led by Dr. Masaru Emoto, he collected water samples from the same source, put them in separate jars, and pasted different words on them. He used this technique to demonstrate the vibrational properties of words found in esoteric beliefs and to determine whether water could replicate these vibrations.

In contrast to the water in the jars containing negative words like hate, loss, and envy, which grew opaque and had malformed molecules, he saw after a few days that the jars containing positive words like love, gratitude, and happiness had structured molecules in the form of beautiful shapes. This occurred as a result of your intention to charge water, which influences its molecules and the universe with an energy memory.

You can simply use the technique as follows:-

- Take water, whether in a glass, bottle, or container. Now, before drinking, you can simply practice ho'oponopono for a few seconds to cleanse it of any negative energy, and then recite your affirmations.
- Or you can also directly take that glass or bottle in your hand or before you and recite your goals and desires in

the form of affirmations in the present tense, like I'm grateful for; I'm healthy, happy, joyful, contented, guided, blessed, and protected, thanks.

- Or you can simply think or visualize about the goals and desires and feel that they have already been achieved and you are so happy, and just after that, you can drink that water.
- Water is believed to have memory, and it absorbs the energies around it very quickly.
- You can also recharge the bottle with positive energy of your desires and goals and then have the sips during the day, or you can recharge the glass of water separately every time before having it.
- Many people also paste affirmations and positive words like health, wealth, peace, blessings, etc. on the water bottle, and every time just before having water from it, they just look at those words and feel about them to recharge water with the energy of the words.
- Reciting your affirmations before water not only recharges the water before you but also affects the water within your body and sends a direct message to the universe about your aspirations. That's why it is suggested not to use negative words, because words have energy which affects you both internally and externally (sends message to the universe).
- Slowly, your belief system gets strong about getting that goal and desire because our brain itself consists of almost 80% water.
- Many people all around the world have unique stories about using the water technique to manifest their dreams into reality.

"This is how you can drink your dreams to reality."

CHAPTER-3

Ho'oponopono -A Magical Mantra

"I'm sorry,
please forgive me,
thank you,
I love you"

Ho'oponopono is a Hawaiian practice consisting of four miraculous phrases "I'm sorry, please forgive me, thank you, I love you".

It is a practice of reconciliation and forgiveness. It involves taking responsibility for one's actions and seeking to make things right with others.

The practice is based on the belief that healing and transformation can occur through the power of love and forgiveness.

By practicing Ho'oponopono, individuals are able to release negative emotions and let go of past grievances, allowing for inner peace and harmony to be restored.

Ho'oponopono, a practice so divine,
"I'm sorry, please forgive me," its phrases align.
With love and forgiveness at its core,
It seeks harmony and balance, to restore.

This Hawaiian forgiveness and reconciliation practice, has a unique and fascinating origin story. Legend has it that a therapist named Dr. lhaleakala Hew Len was able to heal an entire ward of criminally insane patients without ever meeting with them in person. He simply reviewed their files and worked on himself by reciting the four magical phrases by using the principles of "ho'oponopono" to take responsibility for their well-being. This powerful story has inspired many to practice ho'oponopono as a way of healing themselves and others.

This ancient Hawaiian practice encourages individuals to take responsibility for their own thoughts, actions, and emotions, recognizing that they have the power to create positive change within themselves and in their relationships. By acknowledging their own role in conflicts and difficulties, individuals can begin to release feelings of resentment and anger, paving the way for healing and reconciliation. Through the repetition of four key phrases - "I'm sorry, please forgive me, thank you, I love you" - practitioners are able to clear their minds and hearts of negativity, allowing for a deeper sense of peace and harmony to take root.

For example, a person who has been holding onto anger towards a family member for years may decide to practice Ho'oponopono. By sincerely repeating the phrases "I'm sorry, please forgive me, thank you, I love you" in relation to their past conflicts and while just only thinking about the person or situation, they will find that they are able to let go of their resentment and open up the possibility for healing and reconciliation. This practice can help them cultivate empathy and understanding towards their family member, ultimately leading to a more harmonious relationship with self and others.

We can take an another example of a patient suffering from severe trauma and depression was able to find healing and peace through the practice of ho'oponopono. By acknowledging their own role in their suffering and expressing forgiveness towards themselves and others, they were able to release deep-rooted negative energy and experience profound emotional healing. This example illustrates the profound impact that taking responsibility for one's emotions and seeking forgiveness can have on one's well-being and overall quality of life.

How to Practice "Ho'oponopono" ?

Now the question arises that how to practice this miraculous mantra for self-healing and reconciliation. As explained in previous chapters too acceptance is a very powerful step whether it comes to LOA (Law of Attraction) or self-healing through Ho'oponopono.

- Accept that the situation or the condition you are stuck in, is also due to your past karmas or current thought patterns or actions.
- It may not mean or be necessary that you only are responsible for this feeling of grudge and resentment but still accept it from your side atleast.
- Simply think about the person or situation or yourself (according to the case), and repeat the four phrases "I am sorry, Please forgive me, Thank You, I Love You" and repeat again and again until you feel at ease or free of guilt and burden.
- It's a game of feeling, feel each phrase while you repeat the four magical phrases and repeat it until you feel healed and burden free. Remember you will come to

know automatically exactly when to stop practicing via the feeling of ease and content inside yourself.

- It's a sort of cleansing exercise which will cleanse you of your negative energies towards yourself and others and as we talked earlier it's all a game of energies.
- Once you practice Ho'oponopono you will see that you will start vibrating at frequencies of ease, happiness and Joy.
- It not only will affect your energy but also of the other person too by channelizing the energy blocks and cleansing the negative energies and making the conflicts and resentment cleared, fostering a way for happier and healthier relationships.

Ho'oponopono and Law of Attraction

Law of attraction is a game of energies and visualisation. Where emotional feeling of the desire taken as already been completed along with true intentions without any doubt in heart shape energies and their frequencies, which helps propagate our energy into the universe in response to which universe provide us with the same results as desired, into reality.

As Law of Attraction works on energy and frequency principle, Ho'oponopono helps here to set yourself to vibrate at desired frequency so that you can easily attract and manifest whatever you want in very less time.

I find Ho'oponopono and affirmations as the easiest methods to practice for Manifestation and Law of Attraction. How to practice Ho'oponopono for law of attraction? Ho'oponopono is a powerful Hawaiian practice that involves taking responsibility for everything that comes into your life, whether positive or negative. To practice ho'oponopono for the law of attraction, start by acknowledging and releasing any negative emotions or beliefs that may be blocking your desires from manifesting. Then, focus on gratitude and positivity, visualizing your goals as if they have already come true. By aligning your thoughts and emotions with your desires, you can attract more of what you want into your life with the help of ho'oponopono.

Now the question arises, how to practice it for manifestation and Law of Attraction?

- Though it can be practiced anywhere anytime, there are no certain rules regarding it. But it's great to grab a peaceful environment to practice it so that you can focus easily and effectively.
- Firstly cleanse yourself of any negative energy by practicing Ho'oponopono for yourself that is by saying the four magical phrases to yourself till you feel at ease and peace.
- Now, think about your desired goal or visualise it already happening in reality while reciting the magical phrases.
- Remember there should be no doubt in heart while practicing.
- It's a game of energy and emotion, feel the desire as already been completed and visualise it in detail like How People are congratulating you? How you and your loved ones are celebrating it? How you are feeling?, Etc.
- Don't practice too much, stop when you feel like stopping, because too much of practice which is not done heartily shows your desperation towards the desire which will attract further desperation.

An Intelligent Adult

- You will get to know exactly when to stop, your inner voice will guide you.
- It's results are very quick and fast when practiced correctly.
- There's no limit as when to practice, where to practice and how many time to practice in a day. You can do it as long as you want and many times as you like the only restriction is that it should be practiced heartily without desperation.
- The time taken in manifestation depends on your desire and it's nature. Although it works magically but sometimes it may take some time depending on the nature of outcome and your way of practicing.
- But gradual or Fast you will surely get it until and unless the hindering or opposing energies are not bigger and of more intensity than your burning desire.
- Hindering energies refers to the energy put by the another person, materialistic object and sometimes your self-doubt and lack of confidence also works as an obstacle in your way of manifestation.
- But remember persuasion is a powerful weapon to these obstacles.
- what I say always is that contentment has it all into itself, feeling contented and visualising yourself happy, joyful, contented and guided will provide you with everything that you need to feel the above feelings also you can practice for particular desires too.
- Remember, the universe knows you better than yourself.

I wish you a positive and happy manifestation journey.

Ho'oponopono for happy relationships

It just works wonders in the case of relationships whenever there is any conflict, resentment and disappointment with any family person or friend. Simply do Ho'oponopono for that person and you will see the magic, how that person will treat you like normal? and sometimes with more affection and love than before.

It also clutter out the negativities in your heart regarding that person and make you able to forget and let go of the resentment and disappointments.

Ho'oponopono is basically a energy cleansing mantra which cleanses you aura and also the aura of that person also about which you think and feel while practicing.

It cleanses you of all negativities and make enough space for the positivity to enter and provide you with desirable results into a relationship.

How to practice:-

- First of all accept the situation, and acknowledge that somehow directly or indirectly you were also responsible for the causes of the conflict.
- After that, think about the person and think one by one (if it's about a group) and repeat the four magical phrases into your mind or via speech.
- Feel each phrase when you recite it so that it works fast and effectively for you.
- Stop when you feel like stopping or when you feel cleansed of the negativity and resentment, disappointment or jealousy.

- Although it works wonders in just a single practice but it also depends on your expertise to practice. How you coordinate your emotions with your words.
- Practice when you feel like practicing and stop when you feel like stopping.
- Remember no desperation should be there, it should be an easy and relaxed process.
- It's to make you stress free and at love into your relationships not to make you further stressed out while practicing in desperation. So be easy and relaxed, when you have a powerful mantra with yourself.
- It can also be practiced before you are going to meet someone for the very first time, just think about that person in mind or about the perception of that person and practice it for that person.
- It will cleanse you and the other person of any negativity beforehand only so that you experience a charismatic meeting or date.

So next time whenever you have any conflict, angry about someone, jealous of someone, disappointed with someone or feeling any kind of resentment. Don't forget you have a powerful mantra backing you this time.

I wish you happy relationships with really strong and pure bonds.

Ho'oponopono for Desired Health

Along with various physical causes, Health issues happen due to negative thinking patterns, unconscious negative loops, energy blockages, etc.

You may get help in your physical, mental and emotional ailments with the help of Ho'oponopono. Whenever you feel ill or not well whether physically, mentally or emotionally, just simply practice this magical exercise to feel better.

Ho'oponopono clears your energy blockages and washes up all your negative thought patterns and fill you with positivity and provide you with optimal or desired health.

How to Practice Ho'oponopono for Optimal health:-

- ➤ Firstly address your ailment whether it is physical, mental, emotional or related to any specific part of your body.
- ➤ Now, there are two ways to practice Ho'oponopono.
1. **To practice it for getting desired or optimal health**.
   - (a) To practice it for desired health just simply think about yourself or about that specific part of your body in case of the illness is related to it. Now while thinking about that part recite the four magical phrases until you feel like stopping.
   - (b) Or you can visualise about the optimal health of yours or the desired health and while visualising recite the magical phrases and you are done. Listen your inner voice and stop at the point when you feel like stopping.
2. **To practice it to get rid of the ailment.**
   - (a) Think about the ailment or pain or disease and practice the phrases but this time only three " I am Sorry, Please forgive me, Thank you" and visualise the ailment is leaving you and you are getting rid of it. Practice and practice while visualising that it is going away from you, you are becoming free of it, and here too stop when you feel like.

(b) Remember don't recite "I Love you" in this part of practice because you are saying the illness to get away from you or you are sending the negativity away from you, so you can't say "I love you" to it. I hope you got what I want to convey to you.

- Remember there's no limit as how many time or for how long you should practice it. Just keep in mind do it heartily with emotions and stop when you feel like, to prevent desperation.
- There is no need to stop the prescribed medical support and medicines by a medical practitioner. You should do it along with a proper course of treatment. Ho'oponopono will work as a catalyst in your healing journey, to guide you to reach the best available resources and to speed up your recovery and it should never be taken as an alternative to any medical support.

This is how you can get desired health by practicing Ho'oponopono and live your life fully and smoothly without any hindrances.

I wish optimal health for you and your loved ones.

Ho'oponopono For Career and money

Now the another important pillar of human life that is the career and money. Many people are there who are unemployed, many of them are employed but not in a job that is worthy or they are unhappy with their current job.

Now the question arises how to use Ho'oponopono for a dream career. I find it as the most easiest and effective method for manifesting a career of your dreams.

Steps to manifest a dream career:-

- Firstly decide what your career called or looks like or create a perception of it into your mind.
- Now while reciting the four magical phrases visualise yourself doing your dream job, feel that working environment, feel those emotions in your heart, that excitement, that energy within yourself while doing it.
- Be cautious about any doubt that arises in your heart about anything like you may feel that you are not having enough skills required to get that dream job.
- The universe will take care of it, by any source, people or way you will get the qualities and skills required for that dream job.
- You just simply practice Ho'oponopono and visualise yourself into that role and leave the remaining on the universe.
- Don't stress much about How? And When? The time taken into manifestation depends on the nature of your dream job and how efficiently you practice it.

Steps to manifest Money:-

- It's very simple to practice. you can practice it both ways, either by visualising that you are getting promotion, deals, contracts, increments, etc. while practicing Ho'oponopono or,
- You can practice Ho'oponopono while visualising money coming to you from all sides with wings on with how you are feeling? How you are providing to your loved ones with the help of this money?
- Visualise it as long as you want until you feel like stopping, don't get desperate while practicing.

- You will see you are getting money from more than one source, all you need to do is keep an abundant mindset and practice heartily.

Ho'oponopono for Meetings and interviews

Your energy reaches to them before you really meet someone. Remember, it's a game of energy. It is their energy which makes you feel good or bad about someone.

You must have experienced it many times that whenever you enter a room full of people, your energy senses the vibe and energies of that room and you respond and behave accordingly.

The same happen when you meet someone, their aura talks a lot, way more than what they actually communicate. So whenever you are going for some meeting or interview, try this simple technique via Ho'oponopono and make things positive and favourable.

- Before going to meet someone just keep that person in mind and if you have never seen that person before make a perception of them in your mind and say the magical phrases to them heartily, and feel it while you practice it.

- When you will meet that person, you will feel this magic that how efficiently the things are going between you people. This is purely because if there's any negative feeling of uncertainty, fear, nervousness, resentment, anger, etc., they all will be vanished and a positivity will flow in your heart and in the heart of that person as well.

- As Ho'oponopono is basically an energy cleansing exercise which cleanses all the negativities from your heart and also from the heart the person you are doing it for.

- The same will follow in case of any interview, now because you don't know who the interviewer is or are going to be?
- So make a perception of them in your mind and practice Ho'oponopono for them till you feel like stopping, and all the negativities will be vanished.
- You can also visualize the final result of the interview along with Ho'oponopono to manifest it after cleansing all the negativities in your way.
- I wish you luck.

Ho'oponopono For Any Desire

Ho'oponopono for manifesting any desire is a powerful practice that involves repeating four simple phrases: "I'm sorry, please forgive me, thank you, I love you." By taking responsibility for our own thoughts and actions, we can clear any negative energy that may be blocking us from manifesting our desires. By asking for forgiveness and expressing gratitude and love, we are opening ourselves up to receive abundance and blessings from the universe. This practice can help us align our energy with our desires and attract positive outcomes into our lives.

It is important to remember that the power of Ho'oponopono lies in its ability to help us release resistance and surrender to the flow of the universe. By letting go of any attachment to how our desires will get manifested, we create space for miracles to occur. Through this practice, we can cultivate a sense of trust and faith in the process of manifestation, knowing that the universe always has our best interests at heart. As we continue to repeat these four phrases with sincerity and intention, we are affirming our willingness to let go of limiting beliefs and embrace the limitless possibilities that await us.

While taking responsibility for our thoughts and actions can be beneficial, simply repeating phrases may not always be enough to manifest desires. Manifestation also requires taking concrete actions and making positive changes in our behaviour and mindset.

Remember that things will come into reality when you have a strong will and efficient practice with required actions. By any means it has to happen, it may happen by any chance, conditions will be created, paths will become visible but you have to walk, signs will appear but you have to follow, ideas will pop up and you have to notice, people will come and you have to welcome, universe by any means will make it accomplish for you, and that's the beauty of it.

For example, if someone is trying to manifest a new job opportunity, they can use Ho'oponopono by acknowledging any negative thoughts or beliefs they may have about their worthiness or abilities. By repeating the phrases and releasing these limiting beliefs, they can create space for positive energy and opportunities to flow into their life. This practice can help them attract the right job that aligns with their skills and passion.

Simple steps include:-

- Think about your desire or visualise that you already have achieved it while practicing ho'oponopono.
- Do it with peace, feel the emotion of the achievement, visualise in detail and be more specific about your desire.

- Practice it heartily and don't get desperate while practicing, stop when you feel like stopping.
- Happy manifestation journey to you.

Ho'oponopono to heal someone

Often we feel sad about any misery, pain or ailment of our loved ones. We want to do what may be possible from our side. This is time we feel helpless and limited. Through Ho'oponopono you can heal your loved one or even any stranger person by sending them positive energy and love. By practicing this ancient Hawaiian technique, you can release any negative feelings or emotions that may be blocking their healing process. Trust in the power of Ho'oponopono to bring comfort and healing to those in need, even when you feel powerless to help in any other way. Remember that love and positive intentions can be powerful tools for healing, both for yourself and those around you.

For example, if a friend or family member is going through a difficult time and you are unable to physically be there for them, you can practice Ho'oponopono by sending them loving thoughts and intentions from afar. By doing so, you can help remove any emotional barriers that may be hindering their healing process and provide them with comfort and support during their time of need. Trusting in the healing power of Ho'oponopono can bring peace to both yourself and your loved ones and make you able to heal them instead of feeling helpless.

There are two steps to practice it:

1. **Cleanse their negative energy**

   - Think about them and practice Ho'oponopono for them by visualizing that all negativity is moving away from them.
   - Remember you only have to recite it till "I am sorry, Please forgive me, Thank you" because you can't say "I love you" to their negativity.
   - while reciting it visualise that all their negative energies are moving away from them.
   - Stop when you feel like you have washed all their negative energies.

2. **Fill them with positivity**

   - Now after cleansing their negative energies and negative blocks now you will be able to fill that gap with positivity and desired result.
   - For That think about that person and this time while reciting all the four phrases "I am sorry, Please forgive me, Thank you, I love you".
   - While reciting visualise that they are at their optimal health and are enjoying good health with a happy and normal life.
   - Feel their joy within you, feel how happy you are while looking at them being completely healthy.
   - Practice both the Steps whenever you feel like doing it or until the person get his/her optimal health in few days.
   - Remember it may not always work like magic that here you recite and their everything gets solved but by any

means maybe they will get the right place to consult and the right medicine to take through the advice of the right doctor in case of any ailment, but the end result will be, that they will get the good health.

- Caution is that there is no need to stop the medicines prescribed by a doctor or it should not be taken as an alternative to any course of medical treatment, you have to take the action along with trying what right you can do at the right time. Ho'oponopono will work like a magical catalyst and will guide to get you to your desired results.
- The thing is that it will have to happen by any means, people, things, conditions will be the medium to get you to your desired result.
- Happy Healing.

Ho'oponopono For Non living things

We can also practice Ho'oponopono for non living things. For example, if you are going somewhere to work or to live and you are not feeling comfortable in the environment, it may be due to a lack of harmony between your energies and that space. In that case, practice ho'oponopono for that space, and all the negativities will be cleansed, and you will start feeling comfortable in the space.

Likewise, suppose your headphones stopped working suddenly or your spectacles got missed. In that case, you can also practice ho'oponopono for the headphones and the spectacles. The logic behind this is that, as we talked earlier, everything, whether living or non-living has certain energy vibrating at different specific frequencies. Now, in this case, it may be possible that the headphone will start working again after some time, or the universe will show you the ways to make it work;

likewise, you will get your spectacles. I'm not saying here that you do ho'oponopono and the spectacles suddenly appear to you. Remember, medium doesn't matter, but it will happen as you intend while practicing.

It is important to remember that the power of ho'oponopono lies in setting intentions and aligning your energy with the desired outcome. By practicing ho'oponopono for the headphone and the spectacle, you are signaling to the universe your willingness to receive help in resolving these issues. Whether the headphone starts working again or you find your spectacles, the key is to trust in the process and remain open to the signs and opportunities that may present themselves. Remember, the universe works in mysterious ways and is always listening to your intentions. Trust in the power of ho'oponopono and remain open to the possibilities that may unfold.

Ho'oponopono For contentment

Ho'oponopono for contentment and peace of mind. By practicing forgiveness and taking responsibility for our own thoughts and actions, we can release negative energy and emotions that may be holding us back from experiencing true contentment and peace of mind. Ho'oponopono teaches us to let go of resentment, anger, and judgment, allowing us to cultivate a sense of inner peace and harmony within ourselves. Through this practice, we can create a more positive mindset and attract more joy and abundance into our lives.

By acknowledging our own role in creating our reality, we can start to shift our perspective and approach challenges with a sense of empowerment. Ho'oponopono reminds us that we have the power to choose how we respond to difficult situations and that we can choose forgiveness and compassion over anger and blame. As we continue to practice

Ho'oponopono, we can begin to experience a greater sense of contentment and peace in our daily lives, knowing that we are taking steps towards healing and growth.

Steps to practice:-

- Feel contentment within yourself irrespective of whatever the conditions are and recite the four magical phrases.
- Feel that you already have achieved whatever you want, feel like how you will feel when all your desires are completed and when things are going exactly how you wanted them to go.
- Feel that joy within yourself while practicing ho'oponopono, and universe will provide with that same feeling of accomplishment, peace and joy.
- Remember that whatever you ask, will be given to you provided that your will, emotions, practice and actions are aligned.
- I wish you joy.

Note:- People often feel like crying and weeping while practicing Ho'oponopono for energy cleansing and releasing negative emotions. This is a natural response as the practice involves delving deep into one's emotions and memories to heal and let go of past traumas. By allowing oneself to feel and release these emotions, one can experience a profound sense of relief and renewal. It is important to remember that crying is a healthy and cathartic release, and a necessary not compulsory step towards healing and inner peace.

CHAPTER-4

Discipline

What is discipline? , It is a means of instilling self-control and good habits in individuals. It teaches individuals to prioritize their goals, stay focused, and persevere through challenges. Ultimately, discipline is the key to achieving success and reaching one's full potential in life.

The biggest hurdle which comes into way to success or accomplishing dreams is indiscipline, whether you take procrastination, laziness, lack of will, routineless life, failing in execution, these all are due to indiscipline.

We have to keep in mind that days pass, with days those young years of life pass and along with those young days those energy levels and optimal health decay and like this, crucial time of life pass and finally one day the person pass, with goals which were only thought and never accomplished, with plans which were only thought of and never executed, with the ideas which could have changed the world but never came into reality, with expectations which could never have been completed.

Discipline is a choice to lead a life without any regrets.

Lack of discipline can lead to missed opportunities, wasted potential, and a sense of dissatisfaction with one's life. Without the ability to control one's actions and stay committed to their goals, individuals may find themselves constantly falling short of their aspirations. It is important to recognize the importance of discipline in all aspects of life and make a conscious effort to cultivate this trait in order to achieve success and fulfilment.

> *"Life without discipline is just like a ship without rudder."*
>
> -Thomas Carlyle

Discipline is what separates those who achieve their goals from those who simply dream of them. By cultivating discipline in our daily lives, we can overcome these obstacles and pave the way for success and fulfilment. In essence, discipline is the foundation upon which all accomplishments are built, providing the structure and determination needed to turn aspirations into reality.

Without discipline, our dreams remain just that—dreams, floating aimlessly in our minds without ever materializing into tangible achievements. It is through the consistent practice of discipline that we can transform our aspirations into concrete actions, taking deliberate steps towards our goals each day. Discipline requires us to stay focused, to prioritize our tasks, and to resist the temptations of instant gratification that may lead us astray. It is our unwavering commitment to our objectives that propels us forward, even in the face of adversity and challenges. In essence, discipline is the key that unlocks the door to success, allowing us to navigate the obstacles in our path and emerge victorious on the other side.

Discipline can be of two types: internal or external. Following self-control and being able to distinguish between good and wrong are qualities of internal discipline. Conversely, external discipline is adhering to the societal norms. Generally speaking, it is not enough to possess remarkable qualities; one must also be able to manage these traits.

Many people are easily satisfied with little. Nobody who requires control can ignore how actions will affect things down the road. This therefore explains why discipline is a very important life skill. If you want to achieve anything, discipline is the most important quality, any sane person would agree.

It helps you to choose from several possibilities and to follow these options; it also allows you to advance in the way you want. It also lends you the strength you need to overcome any obstacle in your life.

Hurdles in the way to discipline:-

Hurdles in the way to discipline are often distractions, lack of motivation, and a fear of failure. Overcoming these obstacles requires determination, resilience, and a strong sense of purpose. By developing discipline, individuals can overcome these hurdles and stay on the path towards personal growth and achievement. Discipline is not just a tool for success, but a mindset that can lead to a fulfilling and purposeful life.

It is important to remember that discipline is not about perfection, but about consistency and commitment to one's goals. It is about making daily choices that align with one's values and long-term aspirations. By practicing self-discipline, individuals can cultivate habits that support their growth and success. This may involve setting clear boundaries, prioritizing tasks, and holding oneself accountable for their actions. With discipline as a guiding principle, individuals can navigate challenges with grace and determination, knowing that their efforts will ultimately lead to personal fulfilment and achievement.

Hurdles to discipline

1. Procrastination

Procrastination is the process of delaying or postponing a task or decision. It can be caused by a fear of failure, a lack of motivation, or simply feeling overwhelmed by the magnitude of the task at hand. While procrastination may provide temporary relief, it often leads to increased stress and a lower quality of work in the long run. By breaking tasks into smaller, more manageable steps and setting deadlines for completion, individuals can overcome procrastination and improve their productivity.

Causes of procrastination

Causes of procrastination are often rooted in fear, self-doubt, or a lack of motivation. People may put off tasks because they are afraid of failure or success, lack of confidence in their abilities, or simply do not feel inspired to get started. Additionally, perfectionism can also be a common cause of procrastination, as individuals may feel overwhelmed by the pressure to do everything perfectly and therefore delay taking action. Ultimately, understanding the underlying reasons for procrastination can help individuals address these issues and develop strategies to overcome their tendency to put things off.

Procrastination cause negative effect on discipline and productivity. When individuals constantly put off tasks or obligations, they struggle to stay organized and focused on their goals. This lack of discipline can lead to missed deadlines, poor time management, and a sense of overwhelm. By addressing procrastination head-on and developing better habits, individuals can improve their discipline and ultimately achieve greater success in their endeavours.

For example, a student who procrastinates on studying for exams may find themselves cramming at the last minute, resulting in lower grades and increased stress. On the other hand, a professional who procrastinates on important work tasks may miss deadlines and jeopardize their reputation in the workplace.

Strategies to overcome procrastination

It includes breaking tasks into smaller, more manageable chunks, setting specific and achievable goals, and creating a structured schedule to stay organized. Additionally, practicing mindfulness techniques, such as deep breathing and visualization, can help individuals stay focused and motivated. Seeking support from friends, family, or a therapist can also be beneficial in holding oneself accountable and staying on track towards completing tasks in a timely manner. By implementing these strategies, any individuals can work towards overcoming procrastination and improving productivity in their daily lives.

1. **Lack of motivation**

   Lack of motivation affects discipline and productivity in various aspects of life. When individuals struggle to find the drive to complete tasks or achieve goals, their discipline wanes, leading to missed deadlines and unfinished projects.

   Without motivation, it becomes challenging to stay focused and maintain the necessary momentum to reach desired outcomes. Ultimately, finding ways to reignite motivation is essential for maintaining discipline and achieving success.

3. Distractions

Common distractions in daily life include social media, noisy environments, and multitasking. These distractions can make it difficult to focus on important tasks and can lead to decreased productivity.

It is important to find ways to limit these distractions, such as setting aside designated times for checking social media, finding a quiet workspace, and focusing on one task at a time. By minimizing distractions, you can improve your concentration and accomplish more throughout the day.

How distractions can derail discipline

Distractions can derail discipline by pulling our focus away from our goals and responsibilities. When we become distracted, we may procrastinate on important tasks, leading to a lack of progress and achievement.

distractions can disrupt our routine and make it difficult to stay consistent with our habits and practices. To maintain discipline in the face of distractions, it is important to identify and eliminate potential triggers, set clear boundaries, and stay committed to our priorities.

Techniques to minimize distractions

It include creating a designated workspace free of clutter and noise, setting specific work hours and boundaries with others in your household, and using productivity tools such as noise-cancelling headphones or apps that block distracting websites and notifications and modes such as focus mode, DND, Etc.

Practicing mindfulness and staying organized can help you stay focused and avoid getting sidetracked by interruptions. By implementing these strategies, you can create an environment that promotes productivity and allows you to work efficiently without being constantly pulled away from your tasks.

Using techniques like Pomodoro can help to stay focussed and utilise time effectively.

Strategies for Overcoming Hurdles

1. Set clear goals

Setting specific and achievable goals is crucial in maintaining discipline because it gives us something to work towards. Without clear objectives, it is easy to become distracted or lose motivation. By setting goals, we are able to track our progress and stay focused on the tasks at hand ,Achieving these goals provides a sense of accomplishment and reinforces our discipline to continue working towards even bigger objectives.

Along with setting goals practice LOA and Ho'oponopono while visualising yourself accomplishing your goal, feel how happy you are?, How happy your loved ones are?, how they are proud of you?, how everyone is congratulating you?. It will help you both ways at energy levels and on other side it will keep you motivated whole day long and will keep you full of enthusiasm and energy to achieve that goal and to make you feel the same feeling which you had visualised earlier while practicing Ho'oponopono and LOA.

2. Create a routine

Benefits of a consistent routine for maintaining discipline in adults include increased productivity, improved time management skills, and reduced stress levels. By following a set schedule each day, a person can better prioritize tasks, stay organized, and make efficient use of their time. This can lead to a greater sense of accomplishment and overall satisfaction with their daily lives. A consistent routine can help an individual establish healthy habits and stick to them, leading to better physical and mental well-being in the long run.

3. Seek accountability

Accountability plays a crucial role in staying disciplined because it helps to keep us on track and motivated. When we know that others are counting on us to follow through on our commitments, we are more likely to stay focused and disciplined in our actions.

Being accountable to others can provide a sense of support and encouragement, making it easier to resist temptations and distractions that may derail our progress. Ultimately, accountability helps us to maintain a strong sense of responsibility and commitment to our goals, leading to greater success and personal growth.

At last I would like to state that It always take time to leave previously formed negative habits and to adopt the new and productive ones, but remember it's only a game of few days and it becomes your new habit to be in discipline, and you start living more consciously, more living, more accountable and responsible towards self and others, you presence of mind improves dramatically, you feel more living and rather than going with flow you take charge of your own life and can direct it according to your will.

You can also use Ho'oponopono to keep yourself into discipline by reciting the phrases and with it visualising yourself in the desired focused and disciplined state, feel that happiness, that sense of satisfaction and that feel of responsibility. Soon you will find yourself in your desired state.

Quotes from Author:

If we keep fate on side, the only main difference between winners and losers was their characteristic of being disciplined.

With discipline comes perseverance, with perseverance comes consistency, with consistency comes mastery, with mastery comes success.

A men who can conquer sexual temptations, defy procrastination
and keep self in discipline
is capable of achieving anything easily.

CHAPTER-5

The Pomodoro Technique

One of the major reason of procrastination and not able to maintain consistency in work is exhaustion from long duration of work. It mainly happens when a person works or try to concentrate for a very long time, as a result the individual feel exhausted and stressed and then he start procrastinating the tasks.

This can lead to a vicious cycle of avoidance and increased stress, making it even harder to focus and complete tasks. To break this cycle, it's important to recognize when exhaustion is setting in, take breaks to recharge. Incorporating short breaks throughout the workday, practicing mindfulness or relaxation techniques, being hydrated and ensuring proper rest and self-care are essential to maintaining consistency and productivity at work. By addressing the root cause of exhaustion and taking proactive steps to manage it, individuals can overcome procrastination and work more effectively and productively.

What is the solution?

Thinking in tomatoes instead of hours is the key to efficient time management. Though it may appear foolish at first, the Pomodoro Technique has changed the lives of millions of people. In Italian, pomodoro means tomato.

To maintain prolonged attention and fight off mental tiredness, this popular time management strategy suggests alternating focused work sessions (pomodoros) with frequent brief breaks.

What is it, and why it is called so?

The pomodoro technique is a time management method developed by Francesco Cirillo, the then university student in the late 1980s. It's named after the Italian word for "tomato" because Cirillo originally used a tomato-shaped kitchen timer. It involves breaking work into intervals, usually 25 minutes long, separated by short breaks. This technique is designed to improve productivity and focus by allowing individuals to work in short, concentrated bursts followed by brief periods of rest. Many people find the pomodoro technique to be an effective way to stay on task and avoid distractions throughout the day.

By setting a timer for each work interval, individuals are able to track their progress and stay motivated to complete tasks within the allotted time. The structured nature of the pomodoro technique also helps to prevent burnout by encouraging regular breaks and preventing long periods of intense focus. Also the technique can be easily adapted to fit individual preferences and work styles, making it a versatile tool for improving time management skills. Overall, the pomodoro technique offers a simple yet powerful method for increasing productivity and maintaining focus in a fast-paced work environment.

How does Pomodoro technique works?

1. **Set a Timer**: Choose a task you want to work on and set a timer for 25 minutes.
2. **Work on the Task**: Focus entirely on that task for the entire 25 minutes, aiming to complete as much as possible.
3. **Take a Short Break**: After the 25 minutes is up, take a short break of around 5 minutes. Use this time to stretch, get a drink, or do something relaxing.
4. **Repeat**: Repeat the process. After completing four "pomodoros" (25-minute work sessions), take a longer break of around 15-30 minutes.

The idea is to break work into manageable intervals, which helps maintain focus and productivity while also preventing burnout. The regular breaks help to keep your mind fresh and prevent fatigue. Many people find this technique helpful for managing their time effectively and staying focused on tasks.

There are many apps available for free in market to help you with it. Many apps provide you creative interface along with time adjustment facility, where you can increase or decrease the time of your one Pomodoro but it is recommended not to go below 25 minutes.

CHAPTER-6

Living in the present moment

Living in the present moment means becoming fully aware and involved with what is happening right now, without being influenced by thoughts of the past or fears about the future.

Benefits of living in present moment

1. **Reduced Stress:** Focusing on the present moment helps to minimize concern about the future and regrets about the past, resulting to lower stress levels.
2. **Improved Mental Clarity:** When you're totally present, your mind is clear and concentrated, allowing you to make better judgments and handle problems more effectively.
3. **Enhanced Emotional Regulation:** Mindfulness helps you become more aware of your emotions as they arise, allowing you to respond to them in a healthy way rather than reacting impulsively.
4. **Increased Productivity:** Being present helps you concentrate fully on the subject at hand, resulting to better productivity and efficiency in your work and daily activities.
5. **Better Relationships:** When you're totally present with others, you're more attentive and empathic, which can deepen your relationships and increase communication.

6. **Greater Enjoyment of Life:** By focusing on the present moment, you can fully appreciate the experiences and beauties of life as they unfold, leading to greater overall contentment and happiness.
7. **Improved Physical Health:** Mindfulness has been connected with several physical health advantages, including decreased blood pressure, improved immunological function, and better sleep quality.

Here are some techniques that will help you to live in the present moment:

1. **Practice Mindfulness:** Mindfulness meditation is a strong method for enhancing present-moment awareness. It entails paying attention to your thoughts, feelings, physiological sensations, and the environment around you without judgment. Even simply focusing on your breathe for few minutes in a day works amazingly.
2. **Focus on Your Senses:** Bring your focus to your senses—sight, hearing, smell, taste, and touch—to anchor yourself in the present moment. Notice the minute details of your surroundings and the sensations in your body.
3. **Engage Fully in Activities:** Whether you're working, eating, or spending time with loved ones, try to devote your whole attention to the task or person in front of you. Avoid multitasking and be present with whatever you're doing. Multitasking is a scam which costs you of your mental peace and optimal productivity so it's always better to perform one task at a time but fully. Here's too choose tasks according to priority.
4. **Acceptance:** Acceptance is a fundamental part of living in the present moment. Acknowledge and accept

your ideas and emotions without trying to change them. Allow them to come and go without resistance.

5. **Let Go of Judgment:** Practice letting go of judgment towards yourself and others. Instead than classifying experiences as good or negative, simply watch them with curiosity and openness.

    Breathe: Your breathe is always happening in the current now. Take a few deep breathes to centre yourself and bring your concentration back to the here and now whenever you feel distracted or overwhelmed.

6. **Thankfulness Practice:** Cultivate thankfulness by concentrating on the positive things of your life right now. Take a moment to appreciate the small delights and blessings that surround you.

7. **Set Boundaries with Technology**: Limit distractions from technology by setting up defined hours for monitoring emails, social media, and other digital activities. This allows you to be more present in offline moments. Being more engaged with technology makes us less grounded, the virtual world distracts us from the reality. We humans are made up of five elements of nature and getting disconnected from them is only going to give us anxiety, depression and other physical and mental health issues. They say it right that being connected to one's roots is the smartest choice ever. Adapting technology is the need of hour but compromising reality for it costs huge, keeping balance is the smart way ahead.

Living in the present now is a discipline that takes practice and patience, but the benefits are well worth the effort. It can lead to increased peace of mind, enhanced well-being, and a deeper connection to life and people around us.

CHAPTER-7

Ever Living in a state of Joy

In this modern era where we have achieved so many academic, scientific and technological advancements, where society has become more advanced but complex than before. In this fast moving era humans have become more prone to stress, depression and discontentment. Here, the question arises that how to keep oneself in the state of joy and contentment?

Now it is important more than ever to prioritize self-care and mental well-being. By incorporating gratitude and mindfulness practices into our daily routines, we can combat the negative effects of societal pressures and find inner peace. Taking the time to appreciate the simple joys in life and focusing on what we have rather than what we lack can lead to a more balanced and fulfilling existence. In a world constantly pushing us to do more and be more, it is essential to remember to slow down, breathe, and find gratitude in the present moment.

There are few reminders to keep in mind to achieve a ever lasting state of joy and contentment.

- **Listen to Your Heart and Gut:**

    Stay in tune with your inner voice,
    It'll guide you towards a joyful choice.
    Follow what makes your heart sing,
    And happiness to you will bring.
    Trust in yourself, have faith in your call,
    And create a life that's fulfilling overall.

Listen to your instincts and trust that they will guide you towards a path of happiness and fulfilment. By tuning into your inner voice, you can make decisions that align with your true desires and values, ultimately leading to a more authentic and joyful existence. Remember to take time to reflect on what truly brings you joy and fulfilment, and let that guide your actions and choices moving forward. Trust in yourself and your ability to create a life filled with joy and contentment.

- **Surrender to the source/God:**
    Surrendering to a greater force, whether it's referred to as God, the universe, or another spiritual entity, can have great benefits for persons who practice it, the most important benefit is that it kills the ego lying within an individual as he/she accepts that there is the greatest source which governs all. Some other benefits of it are:
    1. **Relief from Stress and Anxiety:** Surrendering to a higher power can bring a sense of relief from the stress of attempting to manage every aspect of life. It can help people let go of worries and anxieties, trusting that there is a higher plan at work.

2. **Increased Peace of Mind:** Trusting in a higher force can create a sense of peace and tranquillity, knowing that one is not alone in battling life's trials. It can bring solace during difficult times and help individuals find meaning and purpose in their circumstances.
3. **Enhanced Perseverance:** Believing in a higher power can strengthen resilience in the face of adversity. It can bring hope and optimism, knowing that there is a guiding power that can help overcome hurdles and trials.
4. **Greater Acceptance:** Surrendering to a higher power typically means accepting things as they are, rather than trying to push them to be otherwise. This can lead to increased acceptance of oneself, others, and the world, creating inner peace and contentment.
5. **Improved Mental Health:** Surrendering to a higher power can have positive impacts on mental health by lessening emotions of loneliness, isolation, and helplessness. It can provide a sense of connection and belonging, as well as a source of comfort and support.
6. **Enhanced Spiritual Growth:** Surrendering to a higher power is often a major element of many spiritual traditions. It can improve one's spiritual connection and lead to personal growth, self-discovery, and a better sense of fulfilment.
7. **Release of Control:**
Letting go of the impulse to control every element of life can be liberating. Surrendering to a higher power means trusting in divine guidance and allowing things to unfold spontaneously, which can lead to greater freedom and peace of mind.

Benefits of surrendering to a higher power might vary for each individual, based on their beliefs, experiences, and spiritual journey.

❖ Protect your vibe:

Nurturing our vibe with positivity is the key,
To unlock a life that's happy and free.

The benefits of protecting our vibe and surrounding ourselves with positive energy include a greater sense of overall well-being, increased motivation and productivity, and the ability to attract more positivity into our lives. When we make a conscious effort to protect our vibe and only allow in things that uplift us, we create a space for growth and abundance to thrive.

By prioritizing our own mental and emotional health, we can cultivate a more fulfilling and satisfying life that is in alignment with our true selves. Trusting in the power of protecting our vibe can lead us to a life filled with joy, peace, and endless possibilities.

❖ Oppose and say no when required:

Don't hesitate to set a line,
Saying no is totally fine.
Protect your vibe, don't let it decline,
And watch as your life starts to shine.

Oppose and say no when required, it benefits us in the long run by ensuring that we are not allowing negativity to seep into our lives. Setting boundaries and standing up for ourselves can be difficult, but it is essential for maintaining a positive vibe and overall well-being.

When saying no to the things that do not serve us, we are making room for opportunities and experiences that bring us joy and fulfilment. Embracing the power of protecting our vibe allows us to create a life that is truly aligned with our values and desires.

❖ Egoless but with a king/Queen like character:

Striving to be egoless, yet commanding like a king,
Is a delicate balance, a harmonious thing.
To lead with kindness, respect for all,
Is the key to stand strong and tall.

Staying egoless while maintaining a king-like character requires a balance of humility and confidence. It means being aware of our strengths and accomplishments without feeling the need to constantly assert our dominance or superiority over others. By focusing on being authentic and true to ourselves, we can project a sense of imperial grace and splendour without succumbing to arrogance or egotism.

The key is to lead with kindness, compassion, and respect for others while also standing firm in our beliefs and values. This way, we can command respect and admiration while remaining humble and grounded.

❖ Value Love, Peace, Time and Money:

Love is about connections, not about possessions,
Peace comes from harmony, not endless sessions.
Time should be cherished, not wasted away,
Money is a tool, not the measure of our day.

- Valuing love means cherishing the relationships and connections we have with others, and making an effort to show kindness and understanding.
- Peace can be achieved by resolving conflicts peacefully and promoting harmony in all aspects of our lives.
- Time should be spent wisely, focusing on things that bring us joy and fulfilment, rather than wasting it on unimportant or negative pursuits.
- Money should be seen as a tool to help us achieve our goals and secure our future, rather than the sole measure of our worth or success.

By valuing these, we can lead a more fulfilling and balanced life.

❖ Try to feel contented whole day long:

When contentment fills your day,
Peace and calm will come your way.
Stress will lessen, challenges won't sway,
You'll find strength to conquer, come what may.

When one tries to feel contented throughout the entire day, they will find that they are more at peace with themselves and their surroundings. They will notice that their stress levels decrease and they are better able to handle challenges that come their way.

While staying present and grateful, they are able to find joy in the simple things and appreciate the beauty in each moment. Overall, striving to feel contented all day long we also send the message of contentment to the universe and in return universe provide us with contentment in all aspects of life.

❖ Do one thing at a time but fully:

> **When we concentrate on one thing,**
> **Our productivity takes wing.**
> **No distractions in our way,**
> **We complete tasks without delay.**

When focusing on one thing at a time and giving it our full attention, we are able to be more present and engaged in the task at hand. This can lead to improved productivity, as we are able to complete tasks more efficiently without distractions.

Fully immersing ourselves in one activity at a time allows us to enjoy the process and experience a sense of accomplishment once it is completed. By practicing this mindfulness technique, we can reduce feelings of overwhelm and anxiety, leading to a greater sense of overall satisfaction in our daily lives.

Whereas on other hand multitasking can actually prevent us from fully appreciating and being present in the moment, as our attention is divided among multiple tasks. This can lead to feelings of overwhelm, stress, and decreased productivity. By focusing on one task at a time, we can approach each one with more mindfulness and efficiency, ultimately leading to a greater sense of accomplishment and joy in our daily lives. The complete engagement in one thing at a time is a type of mindfulness meditation.

❖ **Practice gratitude and become blissful:**

Gratitude is the attitude that brings joy,
Focusing on blessings, not annoy.
With hearts full and minds content,
Happiness and fulfilment are always present.

Practicing gratitude enables us to focus on the positive aspects of our lives, which in turn shifts our perspective towards joy and contentment. By regularly acknowledging and appreciating the blessings in our lives, we cultivate a sense of abundance that can lead to overall happiness and well-being.

As we continue to express gratitude for both big and small things, we further attract the blessings because by showing our gratitude we are giving the favourable message to the universe to get similar and blissful results. By showing gratefulness we obtain positivity and resilience that can help us navigate life's challenges with grace and optimism.

Along with it Living in a state of joy is possible when one is able to practice gratitude and mindfulness regularly. By focusing on the present moment and appreciating the blessings in one's life, it becomes easier to maintain a positive outlook and find joy in even the smallest moments. Cultivating a mindset of abundance and contentment can lead to a more abundant and joyful life overall.

CHAPTER-8

Habits of an intelligent adult

Have you ever thought, What makes a person what she/he actually is? It includes the thought pattern of that person (which is largely affected by the company of that person), set of habits the person follows, and the actions he performs both consciously and subconsciously.

Ideas become thoughts, thoughts become actions, actions become habits and habits create reality of an individual.

Habits of an intelligent adult include prioritizing their mental and physical health, setting goals and working towards achieving them, being curious and continuously learning, practicing self-discipline, and surrounding themselves with positive and supportive people.

An intelligent adult always strives for self-improvement and is open to new experiences and ideas. They also understand the importance of empathy, communication, and adaptability in their personal and professional relationships. Ultimately, being an intelligent adult means constantly evolving and growing in all aspects of life.

In this modern era where there is so much of information to consume, lots of stimuli available easily, fast changing technologies, abundant distractions to waste your time on, where the society expects you to over-perform. In this condition the peace of mind and smartness in actions become a necessity. It is important to prioritize mental well-being and focus on cultivating a sense of calmness amidst the chaos. Here the habits of a person play great role with help of which one can navigate through the noise and make smart decisions and can find a balance between productivity and relaxation

Few major habits of an intelligent adult are:

- ❖ **Reading and knowledge gathering**

    These are essential components of lifelong learning. By continuously seeking out new information and perspectives, we can expand our understanding of the world around us. This not only enhances our personal growth but also allows us to adapt to an ever-changing society. By making a habit of reading and knowledge gathering, we can stay informed, engaged, and open-minded in all aspects of our lives.

    Regular reading and knowledge gathering develops in you the ability to think out of the box and in various multiple dimensions. It makes you able to know something about everything and make you stand out from the crowd.

    When you consistently expose yourself to new ideas and information, you become more creative and innovative in your thinking. This can lead to unique solutions to problems and a fresh perspective on various issues. Your expanded knowledge base can help you excel in conversations and contribute valuable insights in a variety of situations.

- ❖ **Gym and Physical exercise:**

    Physical exercise is not only essential for maintaining a healthy body but also for improving mental well-being. Regular gym workouts help reduce stress, anxiety, and symptoms of depression. Staying active can boost self-confidence and overall mood, making it a crucial aspect of a holistic approach to wellness. So, whether it's lifting weights, doing cardio, or participating in group fitness classes, making time for the gym have a significant positive impact on both physical and mental health.

- ❖ **Good and Healthy Diet:**

People want things that save them time in this fast-paced world, so eating healthy and quality foods has become quite rare. Fast food has become a staple for most people. It's not like there's anything wrong with occasionally indulging in a delicious street meal or going out to dine with friends and consuming whatever our hearts desire. However, it really becomes an issue when such unhealthy ingredients are included in regular meals. In addition to damaging our physical health, it also has an adverse effect on our mental state and level of work productivity. It causes us to become obese, sluggish, and devoid of energy, among many other health problems.

A good and healthy diet helps an individual to maintain a healthy weight, boost their immune system, and reduce the risk of chronic diseases such as heart disease and diabetes, hormonal imbalances due to various unhealthy ingredients in food nowadays, etc.

Other than that, eating nutrient-rich foods can improve overall mood and energy levels, leading to increased productivity and a higher quality of life. By making mindful food choices and prioritizing nutrition, individuals can feel better both physically and mentally and can perform really well in all aspects of life.

❖ **Having a Hobby:**
Whether it is singing, dancing, playing any instrument, drawing, painting, sports, reading, etc. A hobby helps us to look into self and know ourselves better. It allows us to explore our passions and interests outside of our daily responsibilities, giving us a sense of fulfilment and joy. Hobbies also provide a much-needed break from the stresses of everyday life, allowing us to relax and recharge both mentally and physically.

Hobbies also provide a creative outlet for self-expression and can help build confidence and self-esteem. Engaging in a hobby can lead to increased social connections and a sense of community, as individuals often bond over shared interests and activities.

By dedicating time to our hobbies, we are prioritizing our own well-being and happiness, ultimately leading to a more balanced and rewarding life. No matter what hobby we choose to pursue, the benefits of engaging in a creative and fulfilling activity are endless.

❖ **Learning something new everyday:**
Learning something new everyday helps to expand our knowledge and keep our minds sharp. It allows us to challenge ourselves and grow in different areas of our lives. Whether it's a new skill, fact, or perspective, each piece of new information adds value to our overall understanding of the world. By making a conscious effort to learn something new each day, we

can continue to evolve and adapt to the ever-changing world around us.

❖ Diary Writing:

Writing a diary is a healthy habit that allows individuals to reflect on their thoughts, emotions, and experiences. It can serve as a form of self-expression and provide a safe space to unload and process feelings. Also keeping a diary can help improve mental clarity, reduce stress, and promote overall well-being. By documenting daily events and personal growth, individuals can gain valuable insight into their lives and make positive changes for the future.

Diary writing can help you in various ways. It's not only about your day events; other than that, you can write your gratitude journal into it and affirmations into it.

One very important thing I want you people to know is that at the end of the day, when going to bed, most of us think about many resolutions, plans, and things that we want to start or stop from the very next day, but what really happens is that we keep on thinking about the same things at the end of every upcoming day without really implementing them. For example, I'll wake up early tomorrow, I'll definitely study consistently with focus from tomorrow, I won't smoke or waste my time on social media from tomorrow, etc. What actually happens is that at the end of the day, when we evaluate our day, our routine that we have followed during the day, and the consequences that we have gotten, we are doing self-evaluation. On the contrary, when we wake up in the morning with daylight, full of energy, and surrounded by people, we often forget about all these resolutions and goals and keep on performing the same old things like we used to do on previous days. To break these bad habits, your diary can help you out.

Write all your evaluations, resolutions, and goals in your diary at the end of the day, and on the very next morning, just when you wake up, read all those writings. It'll make you aware of all those things, and that too, as the very first thing in the morning, it directly goes into your conscious as well as subconscious mind and will help you to be aware of those habitual repetitions that you want to avoid and the positive ones that you want to adopt.

Slowly, with this simple method, you will be able to break negative patterns in your personality and add positive ones. You can also use affirmations to make the process easier and faster. For example, I'm grateful for: I love studying and I use most of my time in studying; I'm grateful for having very good focus and concentration; I'm grateful for I am enjoying optimal health; in the case of leaving negative habits, for example, instead of saying or writing I don't smoke, try to say I'm grateful for I only follow healthy habits; avoid negative words as much as possible. One more thing: don't forget to say thanks at the end of every affirmation. By thanking, you are making the belief stronger that you have already gotten what you have asked for.

- ❖ **Be self sufficient not selfish:**

Being self-sufficient means taking care of your own needs and being responsible for yourself without relying too heavily on others. It is about being independent and capable, not expecting others to do everything for you. By being self-sufficient, you can contribute positively to your relationships and community while still maintaining your own autonomy and sense of pride. Being self-sufficient is a valuable trait that lead to personal growth and fulfilment.

❖ Day planning and schedule making:

It is an essential tools for staying organized and managing time effectively. By creating a detailed plan for each day, we can prioritize tasks, set realistic goals, and allocate time for important activities. Without a solid plan in place, it can be easy to feel overwhelmed and lose track of time, leading to inefficiency and stress. By taking the time to carefully plan out each day, we can increase productivity, reduce procrastination, and ultimately achieve our goals more efficiently.

❖ Taking care of mental health:

An intelligent adult always take care of their mental health equally as they do it of physical health. In today's world mental health issues are increasing rapidly with so many new mental diseases emerging. It is important to prioritize mental well-being by seeking therapy when needed, practicing self-care activities, and maintaining healthy relationships. Neglecting mental health can have detrimental effects on overall quality of life, so it is crucial to address any issues as soon as they arise. Remember, seeking help is a sign of strength, not weakness.

Doing daily physical activity or any of the sports also keeps us mentally healthy along with being social, connecting to people and family, having good company of friends and having a hobby prevents us from falling prey to mental diseases.

An intelligent adult should take care of their mental health properly as only a healthy mind can take healthy and good decisions and only with a good and healthy mind you can endure the struggles and hardships of life.

- ❖ **Taking charge of their life:**

  Always following Go with the flow is a scam, take charge of your life.

  Take charge of your life and make decisions that align with your values and goals. Set boundaries with others and prioritize self-care to ensure your own well-being. Remember that you are responsible for your own happiness and have the power to create the life you desire. Embrace your autonomy and step into your personal power with confidence and determination.

- ❖ **Not chasing money rather chasing skills and learning:**

  Don't chase money chase skills and learning, money will follow you from different sources.

When you focus on building your skills and constantly learning, you will become a more valuable asset in the workforce. This will open up new opportunities for you to earn money in various ways. By prioritizing personal and professional growth, you will ultimately attract more wealth and success in the long run.

- ❖ **Critical Thinking:** They possess strong critical thinking skills and are able to analyze information, evaluate arguments, and make sound decisions based on evidence and logic.

- ❖ **Curiosity:** Intelligent adults are naturally curious about the world around them. They ask questions, seek out new experiences, and remain open-minded to different perspectives and ideas.
- ❖ **Adaptability:** They are flexible and adaptable in the face of change. Intelligent adults embrace challenges and view setbacks as opportunities for growth rather than obstacles.
- ❖ **Time Management:** Intelligent adults are adept at managing their time effectively. They prioritize tasks, set goals, and use their time efficiently to maximize productivity and achieve their objectives.
- ❖ **Self-Discipline:** They have strong self-discipline and are able to stay focused on their goals even in the face of distractions or temptations. They set high standards for themselves and are committed to excellence.
- ❖ **Emotional Intelligence:** Intelligent adults are emotionally intelligent, meaning they are aware of their own emotions and able to regulate them effectively. They also have empathy and can understand and relate to the emotions of others.

CHAPTER-9
Quotes and poems by author

If one learns exactly when to apply logic
And when to leave on magic
Half of the stress of this world
Had already been gone

Being childlike is adored as
Compared to being childish
Which has to be tolerated

Always be open for transformations,
Opportunities and possibilities
A limited mindset is a barrier in so many
Different ways

A determined mind is so powerful
With unbelievable potential,
Whereas a confused one costs itself
Of energy and time and turns vulnerable

When small things start to affect more,
It's high time you take your power back.

Have patience during hard times,
Because at last it too will fall into place as usual
And something new will airse,
And it's even better to become and unaffected observer
When things look uncontrollable

I don't understand why people want
A scripted life, they expect things to go
exactly their way, and regardless of all the planning
it goes the way it should go.
Life's beauty is in it's uncertainty
All we have is the present moment to focus on

While striving for something big
One should try to make smaller parameters for
Oneself to be happy
Like, isn't it a reason for being happy and
Thrilled that you are alive and likewise for
Countless more small reasons

Your deed will follow you
No matter where you go
Souls don't lie, either your's or their's
Justice is inevitable

Access to worldly information at large extent
Hacks the mind of it's stability
And cause discontentment
This might be a reason that spiritual seekers
Opt solitude as life practice
At the end of every war
Humanity realized that conversation
Could be the solution
The sufferers are not leaders but innocents
The world feels remorse and ironically
Repeat war

The prejudice, comfort zone and
Subconscious patterns need to be
Changed in order to get evolved at all levels

To get high on addiction prevent us from
Being what we actually are, and want to be
We use these addictions as stress relievers
But how will an urge or need to do
Something, to get something will develop
Without the healthy compulsion called stress

What millennials needs to know is
That the number of likes and social media
Stuff should not decide your mood
The real happiness lies within

Our mind allows us to vibrate at any
Desired frequency
We always have the option to choose a beautiful one
Isn't it amazing?

The biggest issue with manifestation is
That we don't tend to have a clear image of
The desired result and also it doesn't
Seem possible until it's done

A new beginning doesn't require
Any special occasion
It happens when you want it to be
It may be now or never

Agitated emotions like anger
And frustration make to flow
tremendous energy Within you
It this energy is utilized and transformed
Properly, Can cause miracles
But if not, will only cause you harm

The person who can look inside himself
The thought process, the vibes, the energy,
The intentions, the urges
He can never get bored and
Every moment is a new exploration

Small efforts made in small spans
Can create big results
This moment is perfect to proceed,
Yes process might be gradual but
Result will be inevitable

Either mind manipulates you or
You manipulate it,
And the interested thing is that
You are always left with the choice

Your heart will take you right there
Where you want to be, just get some
Time for self and simply feel the vibes it's sending

Having good observation and analytical
Capabilities about persons and energies
Are a sign of strong and wider aura

Overthinking is consuming lots of
Energy of youth which is of no purpose
And affecting their overall productivity
And efficiency

Overstimulation caused by internet and
Social media causes lack of attention
Thereafter prevents self seeking and productivity

Addiction prevent healing
It gives occupation to your body and
Confusion to your soul
At last resist the heart from
Being where it really wants to be

To not open up or express
What you intuitively want to
Because of the fear of any type is a
suppression and hence violence to self

A human without being humane
Is like a rainbow without colours

No meaning of a heart
Being rude and blind
It's in need of love
And should act some kind

God has provided us with abundance of
Possibilities, the issue is with the worthiness
What one feels or prejudiced oneself for
This puts limit as well as sets free

Nothing is coincidence, everything
Is a output of many small inputs
Given gradually with time

Everything comes with a price
Person, thing or knowledge
But provided are need to be nice

Those who can enjoy solitude
Are really close to self as well as source
And the rest ones,
They just try to escape from nothing
But themselves
When one learns the art of living
One automatically spend
Moments in meditative state irrespective
Of one's willingness
And that's the beauty of it

The chain of phases
Is what we are going through
Many moments to make it beautiful
Let's try me and you

Talk to him in vibration
Caused by emotions
But with no doubt in heart
And it get accepted

In no condition
Can mind triumph over
The super intelligence
Because human mind has limits
And how can a limited entity triumph a limitless

When one lacks thoughts
Conscience fills the gap
Because nature abhors a vaccum

Human mind provides you with a many
Excuses when pushed beyond it's comfort
And that is where perseverance keeps
Itself on check

Oh dear swan, you fly
You fly in your won sky
Never let them tell you your highs
Yes there comes a hurdle
But you are supposed to try
And in the way, that no space for regret
That you could but didn't try
Oh dear swan, you fly
You fly in your own sky

One thing to not neglect is that
With everything else being available,
Hard work counts

Where the race of mankind for recognition
And approval ends there the life begins

Reality is suffering for most of the people
But reality is simply reality
Nothing more or less
It is actually the fantasization of what
Reality should be which makes people suffer
So fantasy is the culprit
You accept it as it is while striving for
something better
and it won't hurt you anymore
Look it's simple, no?

Solitude can be a great
Opportunity for seekers

Gratitude is one of the
Best possible counters to negativity

Freedom in inner world is the
Need of today
For that you should be brave enough
To break all the false conditioning

Deep inside you already know who
You are and what you want
The problem is that you
Surround yourself with lots of
Internal and external noise
Choose peace for yourself and see,
Answers will start to knock

When we observe and analyze
We come to know that what our
Mind knows is very less
An omniscient and invincible
Intelligence resides within
Surrender to the conscience

When the eternal truth is revealed
Then nothing has control over you

Respect them with love
Who love you with respect

Everything is temporary
Except energy

All that happens it happens
For a purpose
To know, connect the dots of past
See how beautifully you had been tricked
Into actions and situations
And that's how you come to know
Good people, evolved yourself, witnessed
Great learnings, experienced beautiful emotions
So what matters is our approach to it
And that should be positive and optimistic

Believe or not but you are much
Bigger in potential
Than you think you really are

The tough and enduring
Is the hardship
The beautiful and miraculous
Is the learning

Evolve that fast so that
You get to know a new you
Every next morning

Efforts should be put towards
Achieving something significant everyday
That's how you save the day on time

Make them see what they want to see
You do what you want to do
Let the outcome clear all the doubts

To all my folks
I'm here to let you know
Easy is undervalued
For whatever you go
But sometimes it's the most precious too
Grab it or don't regret then,
Because one day you'll surely know it though

As you think, speak, act
This is how you sow
And the natural force starts to work with a go
And then it has to pass in the colour of the arrow
That you shoot with you bow
Often so easy to get and sometimes
So deep although

To not expect anything
From anyone it the key
To self maintained,
Everlasting peace and happiness
And strengthens you as a soul

Choose wiser pre actions
Then a regretted recovery

She looks like a moon
Smiles like a bloom
She sounds like a river
Feels like a cheer
She is like a sweet melody
To which I put on repeat
And just want to hear
To me, she is such a dear

Within me there reside a heart, a soul
Both belongs to you completely and whole

In these fast times where people
Change relationships like clothes
Be someone's wardrobe

Choices are abundant
Opportunities are many
Compatibilities are limited
But worthiness is rare

References and Citations

- Morin, A. (2019, May 30). *Plus: What some people resent about each type of person.* Psychology Today. https://www.psychologytoday.com/au/blog/what-mentally-strong-people-dont-do/201605/what-the-5-major-personality-traits-could-reveal/
- T. (2019, April 24). *What's your blood group? The answer might reveal some interesting things about you.* The Times of India. https://timesofindia.indiatimes.com/life-style/health-fitness/health-news/whats-your-blood-group-the-answer-might-reveal-some-interesting-things-about-you/photostory/69024174.cms
- *Is Blood Type Personality Real? | BetterHelp.* (2024, February 21). https://www.betterhelp.com/advice/personality/blood-type-personality-what-does-your-blood-say-about-you/
- Nittle, N. (2023, April 28). *Blood Type Personality.* Verywell Mind. https://www.verywellmind.com/what-is-blood-type-personality-5191276/
- Kelly, A. (2021, December 1). *A Beginner's Guide to Numerology: How to Find Your Life Path Number.* Allure. https://www.allure.com/story/numerology-how-to-calculate-life-path-destiny-number/
- *Yahoo is part of the Yahoo family of brands.* (n.d.). https://www.yahoo.com/lifestyle/basics-numerology-calculate-life-path-182428429.html
- *These 7 Ancient Laws Can Help You Improve Your Life & Empower Yourself.* (2021, February 22). Mindbodygreen.

- https://www.mindbodygreen.com/articles/7-hermetic-principles
- *Planet: All about planets in Astrology.* (n.d.). AstroSage.com. https://www.astrosage.com/planet/
- Writer-Ish. (2023, September 25). *Do you Need A Disclaimer for Your Book?* Writer-ish. https://writer-ish.com/how-to-write-a-book-disclaimer/

www.ingramcontent.com/pod-product-compliance
Lightning Source LLC
LaVergne TN
LVHW061548070526
838199LV00077B/6953